before the Featherweight

Sewhandy

Volume 1
History

Darrel P. Kaiser

Published August 2008
Darrel P. Kaiser

Darrel Kaiser Books
www.DarrelKaiserBooks.com
email:Dar-Bet@att.net
Green Mountain
Huntsville, Alabama

First Printing

ISBN 978-0-6152-4851-6

Notice

before the Featherweight – Sewhandy Volume 1 details the evolution and development of the *Sewhandy* design, and the influences of society and business on that design.

This book also cover patents associated with the *Sewhandy*, accessories, brochures and advertising.

A copy of a *Sewhandy* owners manual is also included. Always remember to use safety equipment and follow all safety instructions if performing any maintenance or repair.

The intent of this book is for educational purposes only.

No warranty or representation, express or implied, with respect to accuracy, completeness, or usefulness of the information contained in this document, or use of any information, apparatus, method, or process disclosed in this document that may infringe on privately owned rights.

No liability is assumed with respect to the use of, or for damages resulting from the use of, any information, apparatus, method or process disclosed in this book.

See www.SewhandySewingMachine.com or feel free to email me at Dar-Bet@att.net for any additional information or assistance with your *Sewhandy*.

I also provide maintenance, repair, and restoration in my workshop thru my website:

www.SewingMachineTech.com

I welcome any and all discussion as to the "facts" or validity of my conclusions. Specific reference information is available on request; email me at <u>Dar-Bet@att.net</u> .

The Author

Darrel P. Kaiser has been professionally troubleshooting electrical, electronic, and mechanical components and systems for the US Government for the last 37 years. During those years, he also trained with PFAFF in Germany and Bernina USA in the art of professional sewing machine repair, and continues repair and restoration even today.

He has also been researching the development of the Germanic peoples, and his ancestors for over 10 years. While living for over two years in Germany, Darrel "walked the lanes" and did on-site research in the villages of his ancestors.

After all those years of troubleshooting and repair, he turned to teaching at a Government University and writing technical books. Out of his research came his first book on Germanic History and Genealogy, *"Origins and Ancestors Families Karle & Kaiser of the German-Russian Volga Colonies."*

Darrel has also written and published numerous other books on German and Russian History, Politics, Religion, and Ancestry; a book on the Watercolor quilts of Betty Kaiser, a book on basic electrical troubleshooting, a book on sewing machine troubleshooting, two books on the SINGER 221 *Featherweight*, and two books on the STANDARD *Sewhandy* and GE *MODEL A* sewing machines. The last pages of this book show all the titles.

For more on his research into German and Russian History and Genealogy, visit:

www.Volga-Germans.com

For more on his books on Troubleshooting, visit:

www.BasicTroubleshooting.com

For more on his books about Sewing Machines, visit:

www.SewingMachineTech.com

For more on his books about the STANDARD *Sewhandy* and GE *MODEL A* sewing machines, visit:

www.SewhandySewingMachine.com

For more information on all of his books, visit:

www.DarrelKaiserBooks.com

Preface

Originally, this book "before the Featherweight – *Sewhandy*" was written as one volume. After months of research and writing, I realized that documenting the *Sewhandy* sewing machine properly was going to take around 500 pages. For that reason, "before the Featherweight – *Sewhandy*" has been published in two volumes.

Volume 1 covers the history of the life of the *Sewhandy*, i.e. prior to the design (early 1920's) thru the end of production (mid 1938). Also covered are associated patents, identification of your model, a sew-off comparison of an OSANN SINGER *Sewhandy* with a SINGER 221 Featherweight, and parts availability listing.

The original reason for Volume 1 was the recurring gossip and speculation that the Standard "*Sewhandy*" machine was possibly the forerunner of the SINGER Featherweight. Volume 1 was to either verify or dispel those rumors with an explanation using all information presently available.

While writing the original manuscript, I arrived at the conclusion that the *Sewhandy* sewing machine is a remarkable product. The original maintenance manual was not very informative, and some assumptions have surfaced about the *Sewhandy* that are not based on fact, but on a lack of correct information, i.e. required maintenance and lubrication requirements.

Volume 2 covers maintenance and repair of all *Sewhandy* models, mechanical theory of operation, electrical theory of operation, plus advice on buying, restoration, shipping, and replaceable consumables. Also included is identification of your model, a specification comparison of an OSANN SINGER *Sewhandy* with a SINGER 221 Featherweight, and parts availability listing.

The reason for Volume 2 was to provide maintenance and repair information for all the *Sewhandy* models using modern lubricants and components.

Most of the information provided in both Volumes has been verified as fact thru multiple sources. I have attempted to be as accurate as possible; however, my accuracy is directly dependent on the accuracy of all the sources that have provided information over the past 80 years.

A small percentage of the information provided in both Volumes is based on a single source, or my assumptions from a number of sources. Again, I have attempted to be as accurate as possible in my assumptions and conclusions, however my accuracy is directly dependent on information that is 70 to 80 years old.

Note that when I use the term "*Sewhandy*" in both volumes, I am referring to all models of the

Sewhandy to include the **GENERAL ELECTRIC MODEL A.**

If I am referring to a specific model *Sewhandy*, I will add the manufacturer, i.e. **STANDARD, FREDERICK OSANN, GE (GENERAL ELECTRIC),** or **OSANN SINGER.**

I welcome any and all discussion as to the "facts" or validity of my conclusions. Specific reference information is available on request; email me at **<u>Dar-Bet@att.net</u>** .

Frederick and Edward Sr, ca 1933

My sincere thanks to Robert Osann Jr. and Edward R. Osann for their assistance with the research into the history and development of the *Sewhandy* and the FREDERICK OSANN Company. This book would not have been possible without their help and information.

Dedication

There are many companies and people that stand out in the ten year production of the *Sewhandy* sewing machine, i.e. STANDARD Sewing Machine Company of Cleveland, SINGER, Richard K. Hohmann, GENERAL ELECTRIC Corporation to name a few. However, one man stands above all the rest.

Volumes 1 and 2 are both dedicated to that one man: FREDERICK OSANN. He was the Founder and President of the FREDERICK OSANN Company of New York from 1907 until its purchase by SINGER in mid 1934.

He assisted the designer with improvements to the *Sewhandy*, and managed its marketing and production thru the STANDARD Sewing Machine Company of Cleveland.

FREDERICK OSANN became President of the STANDARD Sewing Machine Company of Cleveland in 1930 after STANDARD had financial difficulties. In spite of their financial problems, he was able to continue production of the well known STANDARD Sewing Machine product line.

Even after SINGER acquired his company and the *Sewhandy* in mid 1934, he continued development and research in the *Sewhandy* and other sewing machines thru his partnership with designer Richard K. Hohmann.

Table of Contents

IN THE BEGINNING

Sewing machines had come a long ways by the 1900's, and once they became electric powered, their appeal to the masses exploded. World War I drew women out of their homes to support the war effort, and exposed them to the new technology. The advertisement below uses this theme to promote portable sewing machines.

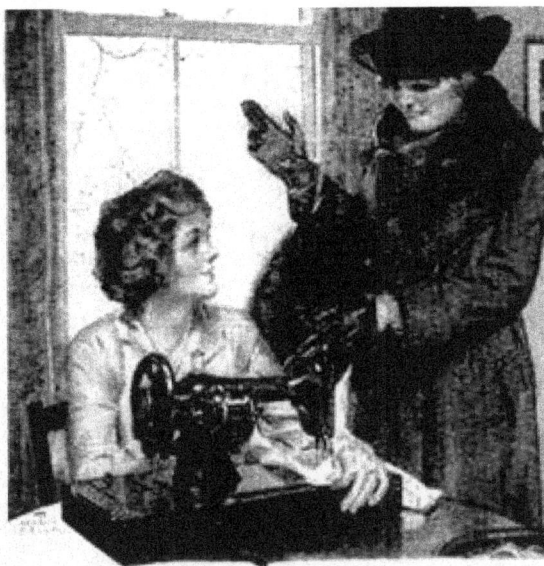

"Why that's the same kind of machine that I used at the Red Cross!"

Thousands of women who helped in war-relief work have learned a practical lesson in sewing efficiency. They have learned that by sewing the new way, with the Portable Electric Sewing Machine, they get a great deal more sewing done in less time and with less effort.

Western Electric
Portable Sewing Machine

Portable sewing machine models were available in the early 1920's from a number of different manufacturers, such as SINGER, WHITE, and STANDARD.

The SINGER Sewing Machine Company filed for a US patent on a portable sewing machine before 1920, and introduced the SINGER "portable electric" 99K for sale to the public in 1921.

SINGER Hand Portable

The SINGER ad below is a typical of the time up to late 1933.

By 1926, STANDARD Sewing Machine Company of Cleveland had their portable model R72 out for sale. Picture below is a later STANDARD portable.

Most of the portable electric sewing machines were just adaptations of treadle powered table sewing machine designs.

For the sewing machine manufacturers this was a logical next step. Add an electric motor and you now had an electric portable model to sell to the public. However, current electric motors were heavy making the machines weigh even more than the table model.

The typical electric portable of the 1920's was heavy with a carrying weight of over 30 pounds. They may have been called "portable," but you would not want to have to "port" them very far.

STANDARD
DE-LUXE

ELECTRIC

SEWING MACHINE

Nationally Distributed and Serviced by

AUTHORIZED STANDARD DE-LUXE SEWING MACHINE DEALERS EVERYWHERE

A new lighter and less expensive portable electric sewing machine design was needed. But for the sewing machine manufacturers the important concerns were:

- ## Who could design one?

- ## Would the public buy it?

- ## Would it make them money?

THE INVENTOR

A new lighter and less expensive design finally arrived in late 1927.

Was it an engineer or designer at one of the big sewing machine companies such as SINGER, WHITE, or STANDARD that came up with the new portable? No! If not them, who else had the expertise?

The new lightweight portable design was the brainstorm of an independent inventor/designer named Richard K. Hohmann (Holmann).

Almost nothing is recorded of Richard Hohmann's early life, other than he was born in Germany around 1875 and immigrated to the United States around 1899. Sometime before 1904 he set up residence in San Diego, California. It was a short time later in San Diego that he started designing and patenting his inventions.

It is unknown where he obtained his sewing machine mechanical knowledge, but he must have had extensive experience. Richard was a very prolific inventor and designer of sewing machine components.

On October 10, 1908, he filed for two patents, 1) on a *Take-up for Sewing Machines* (US Patent 977630 granted 12-6-1910), and 2) on *Rotary*

Sewing Machine (US Patent 983902 granted 2-14-1911).

Four days later on October 14, 1908, he filed for a patent on a *Feed Mechanism for Sewing Machines* (US Patent 957211 granted 5-10-1910). On May 19, 1910, he filed for a patent on a *Bobbin Carrier* (US Patent 1009749 granted 11-28-1911). November 3, 1910, he filed for a patent on a *Revolving Hook Sewing Machine* (US Patent 1000265 granted 8-8-1911).

Three days later on Nov 9, 1910, he filed for a patent on a *Presser Foot for Sewing Machines* (US Patent 1036845 granted 8-27-1912). The next month on December 3, 1910, he filed for a patent on *Take-Up for Sewing Machines* (US Patent 1073489 granted 9-19-1913).

In September 1912, he filed for a patent on *Revolving-hook Sewing Machines* (US Patent 1198546 granted 9-19-1916). On May 3, 1913, he filed for a patent on *Bobbin Holder for Rotary Hook Machines* (US Patent 1105197 granted 7-28-1914).

That same day, he also filed for two more a patents: 1) on *Rotary Sewing Machine with Chain-Stitch Attachment* (US Patent 1090151 granted 3-17-1914), and 2) on *Feed Mechanism for Sewing Machine* (US Patent 1110629 granted 9-15-1914). On July 6, 1914, he filed for a patent on a *Sewing Machine* (US Patent 1164648 granted 12-21-1915).

February 26, 1916, he filed for a patent on a *Sewing Machine* (US Patent 1343823 granted 6-15-1920). On November 3, 1916, he filed for a patent on *Oiling System for Sewing Machines* (US Patent 1311817 granted 7-29-1919).

March 22, 1918, he filed for a patent on *Rotary Hook Mechanism for Sewing Machines* (US Patent 1364279 granted 1-4-1921). On August 25, 1919, he filed for a patent on a *Sewing machine Take-up Mechanism* (US Patent 1393127 granted 10-11-1921).

February 28, 1921, he filed for a patent on a *Bobbin Casing and Carrier* (US Patent 1504242 granted 8-12-1924). In October 1921, he filed for a patent on *Rotary Take-up for Sewing Machines* (US Patent 1549081 granted 8-11-1925).

On February 16, 1924 he filed for a patent on *Rotary Take-up for Sewing Machines* (US Patent 1581346 granted 4-20-1926). On September 22, 1924, he filed for a patent on a *Ventilated Rotary Hook* (US Patent 1596487 granted 8-17-1926).

This list above does not cover all his patents, and there were many more thru 1950.

His most widely known one was his *"Sewing Machine"* (US Patent 1916860). This was the sewing machine that would eventually be marketed as the STANDARD Sewing Machine,

FREDERICK OSANN, and OSANN (SINGER) "SEWHANDY," and the GENERAL ELECTRIC (GE) "MODEL-A".

"SEWING MACHINE" PATENT

On December 24, 1927, Richard K. Hohmann (Holmann) filed for a patent on Sewing Machine (US Patent 1916860 granted July 4, 1933).

The beginning of the patent application reads as follows: "The general object of the present invention is to provide an improved portable motor driven sewing machine primarily adapted for domestic use, and characterized by its compactness, small weight, and good operating characteristics. More specifically, the object of the invention is to provide a portable sewing machine which in respect to its operating capacity, reliability, and durability is substantially as good as, or better than the best motor driven domestic sewing machines in general use, and which because of its construction and arrangement, may be made more compact, substantially lighter in weight, and inherently less expensive to manufacture than any sewing machine heretofore made having as good or approximately as good operating characteristics and of like capacity."

The application continues "My improved sewing machine comprises a frame casting having standard, arm and head portions which may be of any usual or suitable form, and a bed portion which differs from the bed portion of an ordinary sewing machine in that it is of inverted pan or box form. The space provide in the bed not only receives the rotating hook and hook shaft or like under work sewing mechanism and a suitable work feeding mechanism, but also receives the driving motor or at least a portion of the latter, and in addition may receive a rheostat or other controller for the motor when this is desirable."

The application includes seven pages of text and illustrations. What it is important about US Patent 1916860 is that this patent grants all rights to Richard K. Hohmann for all machines of the following type. "A portable lock stitch sewing machine comprising a frame including a chambered bed portion open at its underside, a completely operative work feeding and stitch forming mechanism mounted in said frame and comprising a hook shaft, a needle bar shaft," etc. More description included "A portable sewing machine, comprising a frame casting including a chambered bed portion open at its underside, a completely operative work feeding and stitch forming mechanism mounted in said frame, a base member on which said bed portion rests and to which is detachably secured, a motor mounted on said base member" etc. The complete patent application can be found in the Appendix.

The portable sewing machine design that SINGER marketed beginning in 1933 as the SINGER 221 (later the Featherweight) was included within the US Patent 1916860 of Richard K. Hohmann.

Fig.1

Fig.2

INVENTOR

RICHARD K. HOHMANN

BY

John E. Hubbell

ATTORNEY

13

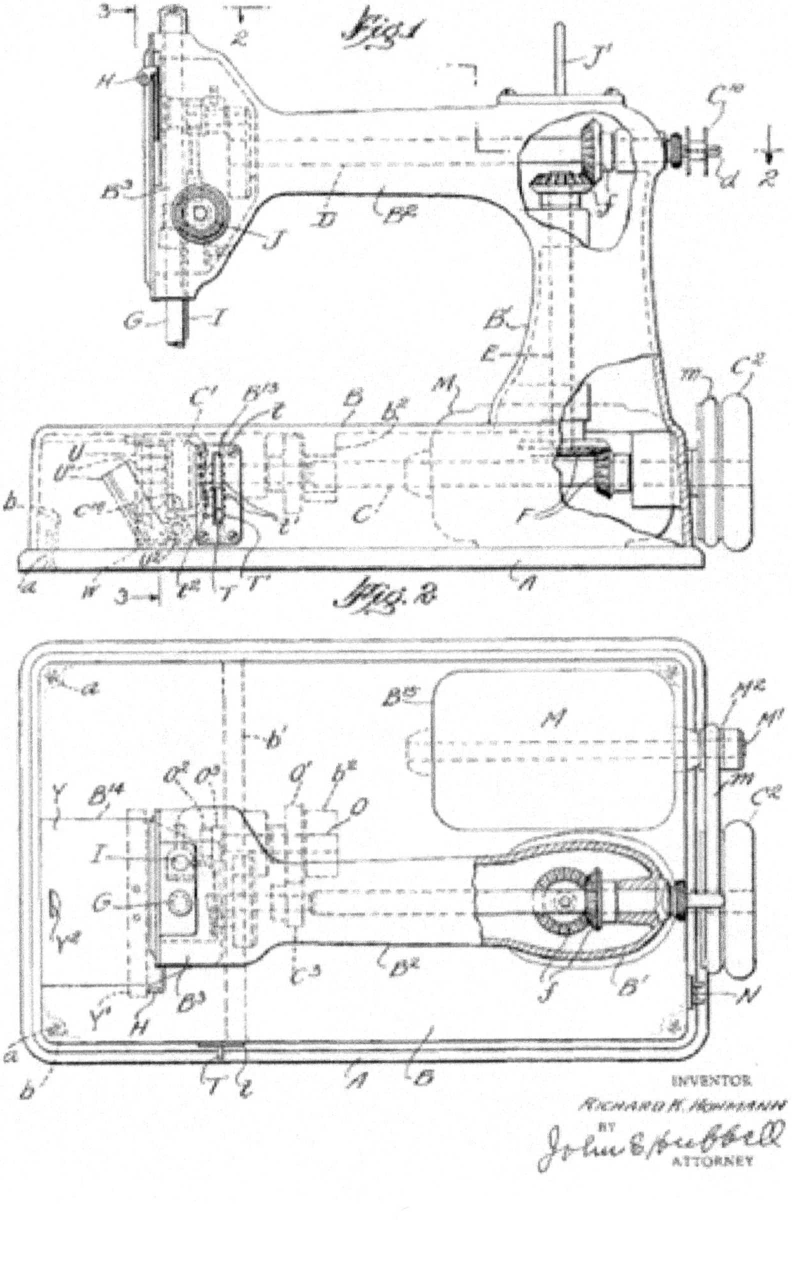

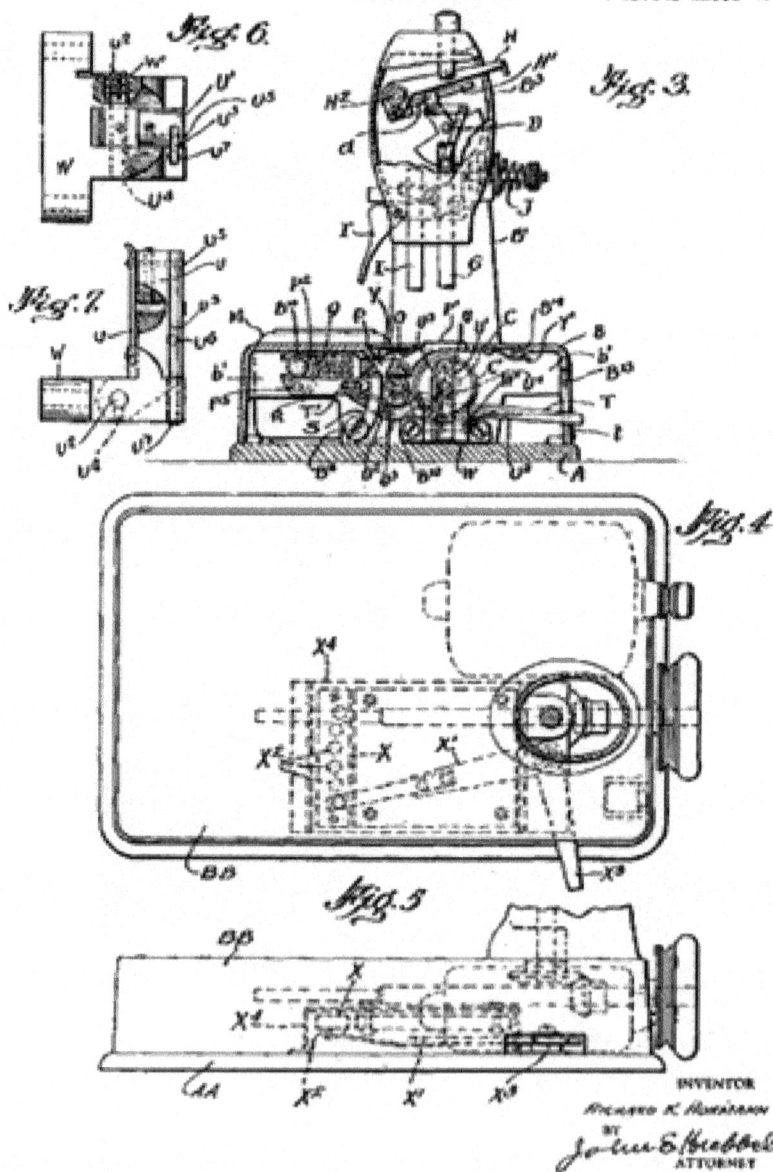

Fig. 6.

Fig. 7.

Fig. 3.

Fig. 4.

Fig. 5.

INVENTOR

Richard K. Hohmann

BY

John E. Hubbell

ATTORNEY

14

MARKETING

Richard K. Hohmann had a new and unique design. What he needed now was a sewing machine manufacturer. Most would probably assume that he went to the STANDARD Sewing Machine Company of Cleveland since that is the manufacturer name that is usually associated with this sewing machine model.

That is not what he did. He contacted the FREDERICK OSANN Company of New York. A contract between Frederick Osann and Richard Hohmann was worked out sometime prior to December 24, 1927. When Richard Hohmann filed for US Patent 1916860, he assigned all patent rights to the FREDERICK OSANN Company of New York. There is no mention of STANDARD Sewing Machine Company of Cleveland anywhere on the patent application.

Why Richard Hohmann assigned all the rights to the FREDERICK OSANN Company of New York is unclear. He was living in Brooklyn, New York at that time about 4 miles from the OSANN Headquarters at 245 Seventh Avenue.

The records do show that he had a past business history with the FREDERICK OSANN Company, and had been selling designs to them as early as October 1922. We also know that he assigned his US Patent 1748479 (Sewing Machine - filed on January 4, 1928 and granted 2-25-1930) to the FREDERICK OSANN Company of New York.

This business relationship must have been good for both parties. Frederick Osann sold the FREDERICK OSANN Company to SINGER in mid 1934.

Was that the end of Frederick Osann's involvement with sewing machines? For more on this, see the section on page 67: Holmann & Osann.

FREDERICK OSANN COMPANY of NEW YORK SEWING MACHINE MANUFACTURER

The FREDERICK OSANN Company of New York is best known for their Osann Fur Machine. This was their foundation product.

The Fur Machine Nameplate

The OSANN Fur Machine – Foundation Product

The Frederick Osann Company purchased many assigned patents during its years of operation. The records show the oldest patent date was July 18, 1907... while the latest was September 22, 1934.

While their primary product was the Osann Fur Machine, they manufactured many others, and were agents for many more companies. The manufactured machines included Union Button Sewing Machines, Union Ticket Sewing machines,

Union Button Sewing Machine Catalog

machines, Union Snap Fastener Machines, *Osann-Standard High Speed Stitching Machines*, Osann Buttonhole Machines, Osann Big Bobbin Machines, Osann Fur Beating Machines, Osann Hat Leather machines. They were also agents for Lewis Blind Stitch Machines, Ballard Electric Cloth Cutters, Individual Electric Motor Tables, Saxmayer Parcel Tying Machines, Chandler Platting Machines, Reliable Fur Drum, Reliable Uncurling Machines, Pinking Machines, among others.

A copy of a business card belonging to Edward Osann Sr., brother of Frederick Osann and Secretary of Frederick Osann Company, is below listing some of sewing machine lines represented by Frederick Osann Company.

TELEPHONES
WATKINS 7596-7597-7598-7599

CABLE ADDRESS
OSANNRICK, NEW YORK

FREDERICK OSANN COMPANY
INCORPORATED
SEWING MACHINES

MANUFACTURERS OF
UNION BUTTON SEWING MACHINES
UNION TICKET SEWING MACHINES
UNION SNAP FASTENER MACHINES
OSANN-STANDARD
HIGH SPEED STITCHING MACHINES
OSANN BUTTONHOLE MACHINES
OSANN BIG BOBBIN MACHINES
OSANN FUR SEWING MACHINES
OSANN FUR BEATING MACHINES
OSANN HAT LEATHER MACHINES

SOLE AGENTS FOR
LEWIS BLIND STITCH MACHINES
BALLARD ELECTRIC CLOTH CUTTERS
INDIVIDUAL ELECTRIC MOTOR TABLES
SAXMAYER PARCEL TYING MACHINES
CHANDLER PLAITING MACHINES
RELIABLE FUR DRUM
RELIABLE UNCURLING MACHINES
PINKING MACHINES
AND OTHER SPECIAL EQUIPMENT
FOR GARMENT MANUFACTURERS

245 SEVENTH AVENUE, NEW YORK

REPRESENTED BY E. W. OSANN, SECRETARY

Edward Sr, Business Card

Early on, the Frederick Osann Company occupied two floors in a 12 story building at the northeast corner of Twenty-fourth Street with an address of 245 Seventh Avenue, New York. In February 1923, the Frederick Osann Company bought the whole building (renamed *The Osann Building*) and expanded its operations.

The Osann Building

Frederick (l) and Edward Sr I, ca 1933

In addition to the original R.K. Hohmann Sewing Machine Patent #1916860, the Frederick Osann Company was also involved with several other patents related to this sewing machine model.

On April 10, 1928, patent application records show that the Frederick Osann Company was assigned rights for a "DESIGN FOR A PORTABLE SEWING-MACHINE FRAME" by Raymond L. Plumley. This covered the "ornamental design" of the portable sewing machine.

UNITED STATES PATENT OFFICE

RAYMOND L. PLUMLEY, OF BROOKLYN, NEW YORK, ASSIGNOR TO FREDERICK OSANN COMPANY, OF NEW YORK, N. Y., A CORPORATION OF NEW YORK

DESIGN FOR A PORTABLE SEWING-MACHINE FRAME

Application filed April 10, 1928. Serial No. 28,215. Term of patent 14 years.

To all whom it may concern:

Be it known that I, RAYMOND L. PLUM-LEY, a citizen of the United States, residing at Brooklyn, New York, in the county of Kings and State of New York, have invented a new, original, and ornamental Design for a Portable Sewing-Machine Frame, of which the following is a specification, reference be-

ing had to the accompanying drawing, forming part thereof.

Figs. 1 and 2 are elevations in perspective from opposite sides of the machine frame.

I claim:

The ornamental design for a portable sewing machine frame, substantially as shown.

RAYMOND L. PLUMLEY.

Dec. 24, 1929   Des. 80,185

While the application states that "a new, original design," it is in the same as the one used by R.K. Holmann in the patent application for #1916860 filed 4 months earlier. It should be noted that design patents were usually granted faster than regular patents. This one was no exception.

While this design patent was granted eighteen months later on December 24, 1929 as US Design Patent 80,185; the original R.K. Holmann patent application that was filed on December 24, 1927 took 67 months (almost 6 years later) to be granted as US Patent #1916860 (July 4,1933.)

It may be that the Frederick Osann Company was concerned about other companies manufacturing the design without paying royalties during the 67 months it took the first utility patent application to be granted as US Patent #1916860.

The Design Patent #80185 is the one that is labeled on all but the very earliest machines.

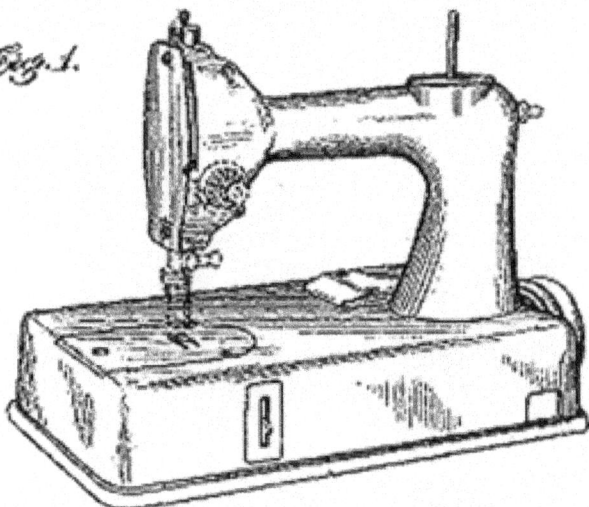

Fig. 1.

Fig. 2.

INVENTOR
RAYMOND L. PLUMLEY
BY
John E. Hubbell
ATTORNEY

On July 28, 1928, patent application records show that the FREDERICK OSANN Company was assigned rights for a "SEWING MACHINE LIGHT ARRANGEMENT" by Raymond L. Plumley.

Sept. 27, 1932.   R. L. PLUMLEY   1,879,708

SEWING MACHINE LIGHT ARRANGEMENT

Filed July 28, 1928

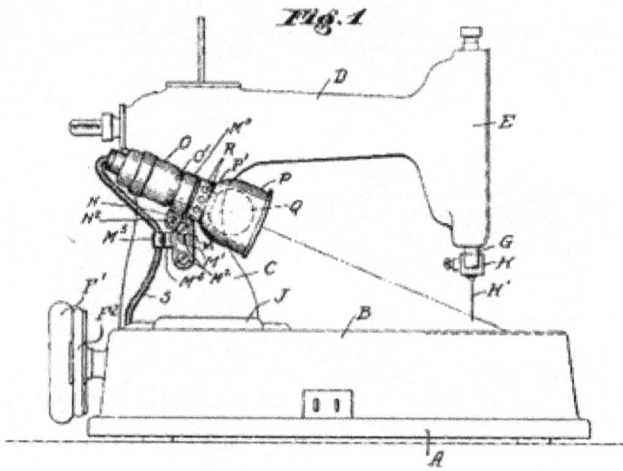

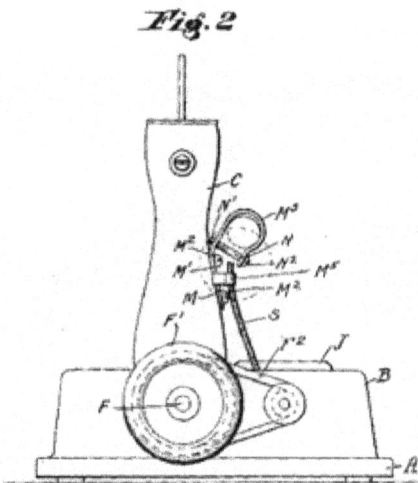

Fig. 1

Fig. 2

INVENTOR.
RAYMOND L. PLUMLEY
BY John E. Hubbell
ATTORNEY.

F. Osann and Raymond L. Plumley applied for a patent on a "PORTABLE SEWING MACHINE CARRYING CASE" May 21,1929. This covered the

Aug. 30, 1932.　　　　F. OSANN ET AL　　　　1,875,177

PORTABLE SEWING MACHINE CARRYING CASE

Filed May 21, 1929

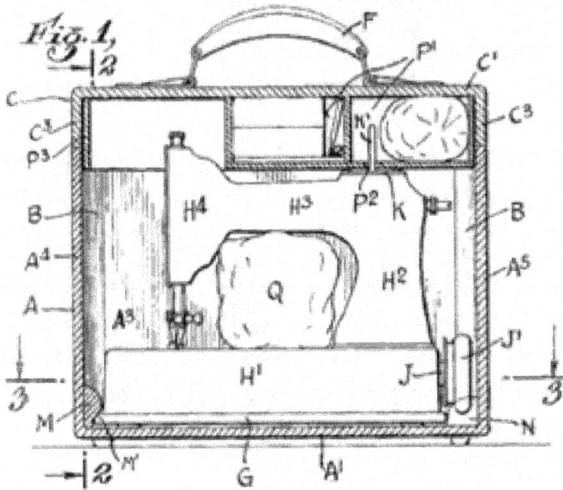

Fig.1,

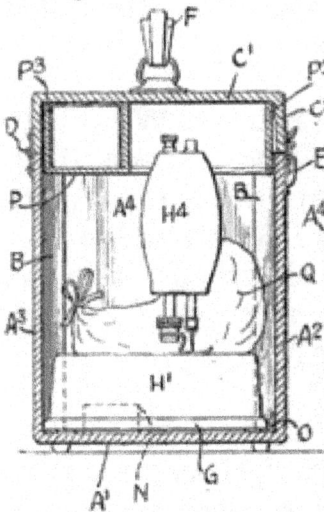

Fig.2,

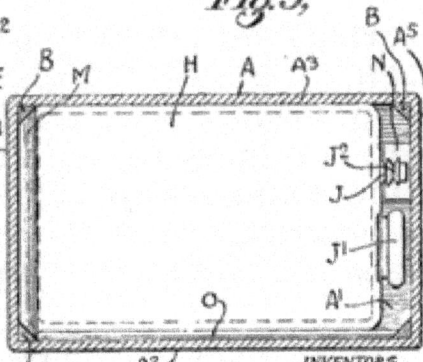

Fig.3,

INVENTORS
FREDERICK OSANN
RAYMOND L. PLUMLEY
BY
John E. Hoffell
ATTORNEY

27

case that was used on their portable sewing machine, and the Singer 221 machine. The records also show that this Patent was assigned to the FREDERICK OSANN Company.

Ok, so what does all this historical information tell us? The accepted idea is that STANDARD Sewing Machine Company of Cleveland was making the "*Sewhandy*" for years before 1929.

Inventor, R.K. Holmann did not file his patent application until December 24, 1927. The patent application for the "*Sewhandy*" design was not filed until April 28, 1928; while the patent application for the lighting used on the "*Sewhandy*" was not filed until July 28, 1928. Last, the patent application for the carrying case was not filed until May 29, 1929.

From those dates, I have estimated that the production of the "*Sewhandy*" machines did not start before March 1928.

This brings up another question. Why did the FREDERICK OSANN Company, who owned all the manufacturing rights to the machine, lighting, design, and carry case, have STANDARD Sewing Machine Company of Cleveland do the actual manufacturing? Was there a prior relationship between the two companies?

Let's look at the second question first. Was there a prior relationship between the two companies? The records are almost non-existent.

However, there is one hint of the two companies previously working together. The business card of Edward Osann Sr., brother of Frederick Osann and Secretary of FREDERICK OSANN Company lists the machines that they manufactured. One of them was the "OSANN-<u>STANDARD</u> High Speed Stitching Machine." From this, it appears that FREDERICK OSANN Company was manufacturing the "high speed stitching machine" for both companies at the time of the business card.

OK, so we have a connection. Still, why did the FREDERICK OSANN Company, who owned all the manufacturing rights, have STANDARD Sewing Machine Company of Cleveland do the actual manufacturing?

My best guess is that it was simply that the STANDARD Sewing Machine Company of Cleveland was better known to the women sewing at home. It had been around since 1884, and it was known and had a good reputation. The name was a household word, much like SINGER (though not a well known). As for the FREDERICK OSANN Company, very few outside of the sewing machine trade or manufacturers had ever heard of it. They were not a "household" name.

For whatever the reasons, the first of these R.K. Hohmann designed portable sewing machines were manufactured and marketed by STANDARD Sewing Machine Company of Cleveland under license from the FREDERICK OSANN Company beginning around March 1928. One interesting note; not all the parts for these STANDARD portables were made in Cleveland. The electric motors installed on all the STANDARD portables were made by the GENERAL ELECTRIC Company. This arrangement would later lead to GENERAL ELECTRIC (GE) marketing the Sewhandy under their label as the GE Model-A.

STANDARD Sewing Machine Company of Cleveland poster

A Standard Advertisement

31

Medallion commemorating that The STANDARD Sewing Machine Company of Cleveland, Ohio, USA, was awarded two gold medals for their sewing machines at the 1898 Trans-Mississippi and International Exposition held in Omaha, Nebraska.

STANDARD SEWING MACHINE COMPANY of CLEVELAND

The STANDARD Sewing Machine Company was located in Cleveland, Ohio, and started manufacturing sewing machines in 1884. William S. Mack and his brother, Frank Mack, founded STANDARD.

Their most popular model was the STANDARD Rotary Machine. It was manufactured almost without change from the 1880s through the 1910s.

STANDARD also manufactured a number of vibrating shuttle models. However, the rotary models were always the most popular with the sewing public.

STANDARD manufactured sewing machines for a number of other companies. Machines would be have a totally different brand name, i.e. one sold as the Minnesota "L". Another was an economy rotary labeled as a KENMORE and sold by Sears Roebuck & Co. in their fall 1919 catalog.

Their machines were advertised as "the worlds best" with a lifetime warranty. While they did make excellent machines, STANDARD may be even better known for the type of advertising it used to promote its sewing machines.

STANDARD produced an unbelievable number of different trade cards featuring their product line. In the early 1800's, trade cards became the major way to advertise products and services in America. These were the business cards of the 18th century, and were attractive, brightly colored cards that could be collected and pasted in a book similar to stamp collecting today.

Their dealers wanted the cards to be viewed again and again, and what better way to do that than make them collectable.

A typical trade card would be about 3 inches by 5 inches with a product picture on the front and full advertising text on the back. The popularity of the trade cards peaked about 1890, and became rare by the early 1900's when magazine and newspaper advertising became more cost effective.

STANDARD was not the only sewing machine company to provide trade cards. SINGER also produced a wide variety promoting their sewing machines.

Other sewing machine companies such as HOWE, WHITE, McLEAN and HOOPER, AMERICAN, WILCOX and GIBBS, WHEELER and WILSON, and WEED also used this type of advertising.

Copies of six STANDARD trade cards are included on the next two pages.

NATURE'S KINDERGARTEN

KEEP OFF THE GRASS AND BUY A STANDARD SEWING MACHINE

THE NATION'S PRIDE
THE STANDARD ROTARY SHUTTLE SEWING MACHINE

Compliments of THE STANDARD SEWING MACHINE CO.
CLEVELAND, OHIO

Compliments of the STANDARD SEWING MACHINE CO. CLEVELAND O

THE OLD AND THE NEW

STANDARD CENTRAL NEEDLE SEWING MACHINE
Be Sure to Investigate Before You Buy
THE STANDARD SEWING MACHINE CO. CLEVELAND OHIO U.S.A.

"THE STANDARD" OUR NAME IS OUR MOTTO.
3000 TURNS IN A MINUTE. CLEAR THE TRACK.
STANDARD
ROTARY SHUTTLE
COMPLIMENTS OF
THE STANDARD SEWING MACHINE CO.
CLEVELAND, O.
THE STANDARD ROTARY SHUTTLE SEWING MACHINE.
THE LIGHTEST, QUIETEST, SWIFTEST,
RUNNING MACHINE IN THE WORLD.
AGENT.

THE NATION'S PRIDE
THE STANDARD OF CONQUEST
PRESENTED BY THE STANDARD SEWING MACHINE CO.
CLEVELAND OHIO

As noted above, William S. Mack and his brother, Frank Mack, founded the STANDARD SEWING MACHINE COMPANY.

William A. Mack was born in Portage, New York. He began to work with sewing machines in 1861, and patented a sewing machine design in 1863. This was the basic design for the machines manufactured by his company, the DOMESTIC Sewing machine Company.

W. A. Mack

As DOMESTIC grew, he moved from Cleveland and to Norwalk for increased space. He was so successful in building sales that other sewing machine companies attempted to suppress the machine.

Success required more financing, and the involvement of other investors and eastern capitalists as stockholders. In 1869, when DOMESTIC incorporated, William and his brother, Frank, both became stockholders in the new corporation.

Majority control of the "new" DOMESTIC was with the eastern capitalists. They decided in 1870 to have the Providence Tool Company, of Providence, Rhode Island, make the DOMESTIC sewing machines for the next three years. In 1873 the DOMESTIC purchased extensive works in Newark, New Jersey. While William and Frank had lost control of the company, they did have design and technical input to the product line.

In the spring of 1884, William and his brother, Frank, withdrew from the Domestic Company in Toledo. William found more investors and with their money organized the STANDARD Sewing Machine Company in Cleveland. Starting over, he attempted to design a sewing machine that "embodied more advantages than any that had before appeared." He was successful and the result was the first STANDARD Sewing Machine.

William's brother, Frank, was born in Livingston County, New York. Frank went to work as a salesman at DOMESTIC in the spring of 1866. The two brothers formed a partnership in late 1866. Frank was made General Manger of Sales of the DOMESTIC Sewing Machine Company. In 1869, when DOMESTIC incorporated, both William and Frank became stockholders in the new corporation. As noted above, both William and Frank, withdrew from the Domestic Company in Toledo in early 1884.

Frank Mack

William and Frank Mack built the STANDARD Sewing Machine Company into huge success. Below is an image of their factory in Cleveland.

WHERE THE STANDARD IS MADE

THE STANDARD SEWING MACHINE CO'S FACTORY, CLEVELAND, OHIO, U.S.A.

STANDARD'S success was not because they were the biggest, SINGER was. It was not because they were the best at advertising or product placement, again SINGER was. Their success came from their devotion to quality and their innovative designs.

The following excerpt is from one of their Catalogs of STANDARD Sewing Machines: "The stitch making quality is the principle upon which all Sewing Machine Mechanism is based, and this principle must be the foundation upon which all

Sewing machines are made. If the principle is faulty the foundation is weak, and the machine must necessarily fail of accomplishing all that was intended. The principle embodied in the standard is the Rotary Shuttle which has been found to contain all the quantities of a Perfect Stitch Making Mechanism; combining simplicity with the ease with which it handles all kinds of thread, it is susceptible of being run at high speed with less friction, less strain, and consequently less wear than machines made on any other plan." They were so sure of their quality they offered a lifetime warranty.

One of their innovative designs (Sitstraight) is advertised below.

New "Sit-Straight" Standard
Vibrator
No. 94½-V

Lifetime Guarantee with Every
"Standard" Machine
Complete Set of Nickeled Steel
Attachments

Automatic Lift (Open)

THE popular round end woodwork so much in
demand, finished in quarter-sawed selected
Golden Oak, hand polished, piano finished. Well
and strongly made and a model that fits in well
with any household furniture. In this style you
have every known improvement in up-to-date
designing.

*Standard "Sit-Straight" Machines Give You More
Room Between Stand Legs Than Any
Other Make*

12

Ad for the Model 94½-V Treadle

The *"Sewhandy"*

The STANDARD Sewing Machine Company, under license from the FREDERICK OSANN Company, began manufacturing the *"Sewhandy"* machines around March 1928.

The first 1100 machines (maybe more) did not carry the label *"Sewhandy"* on the sewing machine neck, but were labeled Standard Sewing Machine. The picture below of shows this STANDARD Sewing Machine logo. These machines also had a simple STANDARD winged logo (Cleveland U.S.A below) on the center of the bed. For more on this model, see page 109.

Early Winged Logo

On August 8, 1928, the labeling changed Standard Sewing Machine with *"Sewhandy"* below it. This was the first use of the *"Sewhandy"* label. These machines had a STANDARD winged logo (Cleveland U.S.A above) on the center of the bed. For more on this model, see page 109.

Later Winged Logo

Eventually, the Standard Sewing Company name was removed leaving only the *"Sewhandy"* as the machine label. The picture below of shows the "Sewhandy" label. These machines had a STANDARD winged logo (Cleveland U.S.A above) on the center of the bed. For more on this model, see page 109.

The STANDARD sewing machines were the 11¾ pound machines with aluminum beds. The FREDERICK OSANN Company later changed the Sewhandy design to cast iron (and 15¾ pounds),

During the first year, the Sewhandy was produced in four different colors: Black, Green, Blue, and Rose. For more on the details and features of the different models of the STANDARD Sewhandy, see page 109.

The End of STANDARD

Something happened to the Standard Sewing Machine Company of Cleveland in late 1929. Maybe it was the Fall of the Stock Market or maybe something else. In any case, information on it just stops.

Issued September 23, 1930 to The Singer Manufacturing Company, of Elizabeth, New Jersey, a corporation of New Jersey.

UNITED STATES PATENT OFFICE

THE STANDARD SEWING MACHINE COMPANY, OF CLEVELAND, OHIO

ACT OF FEBRUARY 20, 1905

Application filed May 25, 1926. Serial No. 231,128.

SEWHANDY

STATEMENT

To the Commissioner of Patents:

The Standard Sewing Machine Company, a corporation, duly organized under the laws of the State of Ohio, and having its principal office at Cedar Avenue at East 64th Street, Cleveland, Ohio, has adopted and used the trade-mark shown in the accompanying drawing, for SEWING MACHINES AND SEWING-MACHINE NEEDLES, in Class 23, Cutlery, machinery, and tools, and parts thereof, and presents herewith five specimens showing the trade-mark as actually used by applicant upon the goods, and requests that the same be registered in the United States Patent Office in accordance with the act of February 20, 1905, as amended. This trademark has been continuously used and applied to sewing machines in applicant's business since August 5, 1908, and to sewing machine needles in applicant's business since January

5, 1926. The trade-mark is applied or affixed to sewing machines by affixing metallic name plates or printed labels on which the trade-mark is shown thereon or by directly printing the trade-mark or otherwise directly printing the trade-mark on the packages containing the same.

The undersigned hereby appoints John R. Truncll, whose post office address is 2 West 45th Street, New York city, its attorney, to prosecute this application for registration, with full power of substitution and revocation, to make alterations and amendments therein, to receive the certificate, and to transact all business in the Patent Office connected therewith.

THE STANDARD SEWING

MACHINE COMPANY,

By FREDERICK CRANE,

President.

The last Standard Sewing Machine patent listed is US1596369 on 17 Aug 1926.

STANDARD SEWING MACHINE COMPANY FAILURE

The SINGER Sewing Machine Company lists on its website that it acquired the STANDARD Sewing Machine Company in 1929. This information is contradicted by US Patent Office records that show Frederick Osann as the President of the STANDARD Sewing Machine Company on May 29, 1930 (see next previous page).

US Trademark Records also that on May 29, 1930 the "Sewhandy" trademark belonged to the STANDARD SEWING MACHINE COMPANY, THE CORPORATION OHIO CEDAR AVENUE AT EAST 65TH STREET CLEVELAND OHIO, not the SINGER Sewing Machine Company. Records also show that SINGER did not buy out the FREDERICK OSANN Company until mid 1934, and it did not record its new creation, The Osann Corporation, until March 11, 1935. Either the US Government records are wrong or the SINGER website is mistaken.

What did happen was that since STANDARD was no longer financially solvent, the FREDERICK OSANN Company took back the license and patent rights on the "Sewhandy" and began producing them in Cleveland and eventually Boston under the STANDARD Sewing Machine Company of Cleveland label. Apparently, the

FREDERICK OSANN Company still believed that the STANDARD name was a good brand with the sewing public even though it was already out of business. Government records indicate that by May 29, 1930, Frederick Osann was both the President of the FREDERICK OSANN Company and the STANDARD Sewing Machine Company (with all its assets and debts).

Registered Sept. 23, 1930

Trade-Mark 275,403

Renewed September 23, 1950 to The Singer Manufacturing Company, of Elizabeth, New Jersey, a corporation of New Jersey.

UNITED STATES PATENT OFFICE

THE STANDARD SEWING MACHINE COMPANY, OF CLEVELAND, OHIO

ACT OF FEBRUARY 20, 1905

Application filed May 29, 1930. Serial No. 301,720.

SEWHANDY

STATEMENT

To the Commissioner of Patents:

The Standard Sewing Machine Company, a corporation duly organized under the laws of the State of Ohio, and having its principal offices at Cedar Avenue at East 65th Street, Cleveland, Ohio, has adopted and used the trade-mark shown in the accompanying drawing, for SEWING MACHINES AND SEWING-MACHINE NEEDLES, in Class 23, Cutlery, machinery, and tools, and parts thereof, and presents herewith five specimens showing the trade-mark as actually used by applicant upon the goods, and requests that the same be registered in the United States Patent Office in accordance with the act of February 20, 1905, as amended. The trade-mark has been continuously used and applied to sewing machines in applicant's business since August 8, 1928, and to sewing-machine needles in applicant's business since January

2, 1929. The trade-mark is applied or affixed to sewing machines by affixing metallic name plates or printed labels on which the trade-mark is shown thereon or by decalcomania transfers and to sewing machine needles by printing the trade-mark on the packages containing the same.

The undersigned hereby appoints John E. Hubbell, whose post office address is 8 West 40th Street, New York city, its attorney, to prosecute this application for registration, with full powers of substitution and revocation, to make alterations and amendments therein, to receive the certificate, and to transact all business in the Patent Office connected therewith.

THE STANDARD SEWING
MACHINE COMPANY,
By FREDERICK OSANN,
President.

48

FREDERICK OSANN COMPANY of NEW YORK
SEWHANDY

The next *Sewhandy* machines are those manufactured by the FREDERICK OSANN Company, a corporation of New York. Do not confuse this with the later OSANN Corporation - SINGER, a corporation of Pennsylvania.

These *Sewhandy* sewing machines were manufactured from mid 1929 until early 1932. Because of continuing manufacturing during the transition, it is not possible to tell where the last STANDARD *Sewhandy* model stops and the first FREDERICK OSANN Company *Sewhandy* begins.

The FREDERICK OSANN Company early *Sewhandy* machines also had aluminum beds weighing 11 ¾ pounds.

Other details follow:

1) The machines came in four colors: Marine Blue, Larch Green, French Maroon, and Velvet Black.

2) There is a STANDARD Sewing Machine Company logo with Cleveland U.S.A. above the wings in the center of the machine bed.

The Frederick Osann Company did make some changes to the *Sewhandy* design. In January 1931, they patented and introduced a newer improved Feed Dog design that reduced the linkage wear. In mid 1932, they changed from aluminum beds to cast-iron beds. This increased the *Sewhandy* weight by 3 pounds to 15¾ pounds. This change was most likely to reduce manufacturing costs. (If a magnet is attracted to your *Sewhandy* bed, then you have one made with cast-iron after this change. If a magnet is not attracted to the bed, you have an aluminum one made before this change). For more on this model, see page 119.

"America's" Finest Electric Portable

Sewing Machines
Sewhandy

manufactured by the Standard Sewing Machine Co.
10 Real Reasons "Why"—You "Will Like the Sewhandy" Portable Electric

Its Weight is only 12 pounds—

It will sew a thousand stitches a minute—

It will not pucker on Chiffon—

It will not clog in the bobbin case—

It will not vibrate a walk—

It is a Rotary Machine—

It is as near fool proof as a Machine can be made—

It makes a perfect stitch—

It is gear driven with General Electric motor and has a sewing light—

It comes in four colors, Green, Blue, Rose and Black—

We Will Allow You $20 for Your Used Hand Run Sewing Machine In Trade On This Beautiful

PORTABLE ELECTRIC

July 10, 1929

The Frederick Osann Company tried to create a sales network for the *Sewhandy*, but it appears that the financial times were just too bad for it too succeed. The following brochures were sent out in 1929 to create interest in selling the *Sewhandy*.

Sewhandy
Electric Sewing Machine
"Portable Without A Porter"

A WONDERFUL OPPORTUNITY

For Earnest and Ambitious Sales Managers Who Want Permanent Work and Big Yearly Incomes

To Men Who Think and Act In Terms of Big Success:

This is without doubt one of the most unusual business opportunities ever brought to your attention. It is only for ambitious, clean-cut men who want to accomplish big things and earn big incomes. We have nothing to offer men of the "lazybones" type who eat breakfast in bed and spend their golden hours in idle dreams and schemes to get rich without working.

This proposition is free from all elements of buncombe, shallow pretense, false promises and exaggerated claims. It has the soundness and honesty which invite your thorough investigation. If you have made less money in the past than you want to make in the future, this is your opportunity to secure valuable territory and handle sales of the new SEWHANDY Portable Electric Sewing Machine. By acting as General Distributor or District Agent and putting head, heart and hustle into your work, you will be assured unlimited earnings.

Home women who are enlightened to their best interests now demand a light and compact sewing machine that can be carried and used anywhere. The SEWHANDY fulfills their idea of the ideal machine. It is completely equipped with motor and attachments and weighs but 12 pounds. It is a midget in size but a giant in service. Every form of sewing previously done on big, heavy and noisy machines is now done quicker and better on the SEWHANDY.

The market for the SEWHANDY does not need to be created, as it has always existed. Ever since the first big sewing machine was made for home use, there has been increasing need of a smaller and better one. Now the SEWHANDY gives you a free and wide-open field for profitable sales. It is new—a real innovation! It is the only portable machine that is light to carry and use anywhere to lighten all sewing tasks.

Read every word of this folder. Consider the high character of this business offering. If you then decide to take advantage of this rare opportunity, we'll welcome your application to serve as an important factor of our sales organization.

(Signed) *Frederick Osann*

President
Standard Sewhandy Sales Division
Frederick Osann Company

© 1931—Frederick Osann Company

53

54

GENERAL ELECTRIC MODEL-A SEWING MACHINE

In June 1931, Frederick Osann (STANDARD) contractually agreed to sell 5,000 *Sewhandy* machines to GENERAL ELECTRIC (GE). These 5,000 machines would bear the GE label (*MODEL A*) and be sold thru the GE sales network.

Later GE Model A

One of the more important parts of the arrangement was that it was agreed that no more machines (after the 750 currently in production) would be marketed as *Sewhandy* while GENERAL ELECTRIC was marketing their *MODEL A*. So it appears while the *Sewhandy* continued to be available after that, it was most likely labeled as a GENERAL ELECTRIC *MODEL A* and not a *Sewhandy*.

This agrees with my research that shows many *Sewhandy* newspaper ads in 1929 thru 1932, but none after that. On the flip side, GENERAL ELECTRIC *MODEL A* ads show-up beginning in 1932 and run thru mid 1935. For more on the advertising see page 127.

You Must See This Perfect Little Jewel

General Electric Sewing Machine

$76.50

Really Portable 13½ Pounds

Use Our Easy Payment Plan

Ask for a Home Demonstration

Really something radically new in an all-electric really portable sewing machine. You must see it SEW... anything or everything...without adjustment. SWIFT ... VIBRATIONLESS. First Floor.

CAPWELL-SULLIVAN & FURTH

April 19, 1932

Because of the marketing and distribution agreement with GE on June 24, 1931, *Sewhandy* marketing slowly disappeared. All of the production beginning in early 1932 was labeled "GENERAL ELECTRIC (GE) *MODEL A*". This arrangement continued until SINGER acquired the FREDERICK OSANN Company in 1934.

The original Sewhandy contract between GE and Osann was 10 pages long (with Covers). Three of the more interesting pages follow:

TO Standard Sewing Machine Co.,   Req. No. MD - 4190
       Cleveland, Ohio.

                                          Date   6/25/31

Ship the following, Via: BEST WAY

TO   AS RELEASED BY SHIPPING REQUISITIONS TO FOLLOW.

Mark packages   MD - 4190   Wanted at destination   AT ONCE

Quantity	Articles

5000-   PORTABLE SEWING MACHINES

                      ABOVE TO BE FURNISHED IN ACCORDANCE WITH TERMS

                      OF CONTRACT 6/24/31.

Contract Page 1

GENERAL   ELECTRIC
COMPANY

1285 Boston Ave.
BRIDGEPORT   CONN.
June 24, 1931

Mr. Frederick Osann, President,
Frederick Osann Company,
245 Seventh Avenue,
New York City.

Dear Mr. Osann:

Mr. C. E. Wilson, Vice President, has executed the agreement between the General Electric Company, The Standard Sewing Machine Company, and the Frederick Osann Company, and I am handing a copy of the same to Mr. Bublitz for your files.

After a discussion with Mr. Bublitz, Mr. Wilson has executed this agreement with the understanding that the price of $25.30 each, mentioned under #1-c, is the maximum price, in case we place orders beyond the first 5,000 and that if, due to the size of future orders or due to economies in manufacture, reductions are made in your manufacturing cost, consideration will be given to the subject of making us a lower figure than the above mentioned price of the machine.

If there is any increase or decrease in the price of the motor, it is understood that the price of the machines to us will be increased or reduced by a like amount.

I am sending you this letter in duplicate and, if the above meets with your approval, will you kindly sign a copy and return it to me for my files?

Yours very truly,

(Signed) Howard R. Sargent

Engineer, Merchandise Dept.

HRS'G
Approved: FREDERICK OSANN COMPANY
THE STANDARD SEWING MACHINE COMPANY

By: _____
President

Contract Page 2

58

WHEREAS, the General Company is desirous of purchasing certain portable sewing machines for resale, and of acquiring certain exclusive rights to sell such machines, and is also desirous of obtaining an option to acquire exclusive license rights to manufacture and sell said portable sewing machine and to acquire certain facilities for such manufacture;

NOW, THEREFORE, the parties have agreed together as follows:

1. The Standard Company will manufacture and sell, and the General Company will buy five-thousand (5,000) portable sewing machines, attachments and carrying cases according to the following terms and conditions:

(a) The Standard Company will deliver F.O.B. Cleveland, Ohio, and final deliveries shall be completed approximately within three (3) months from September 1st, 1931. Shipments shall be made as specified by the General Company to its distributors. Neither party shall be liable for delays resulting from causes beyond its control or caused by fire, strike, civil or military authority.

(b) With respect to all parts of said portable machines, except the electrical parts to be furnished by the General Company as hereinafter specified, the Standard Company gives the following warranties:

The said machines shall be in all respect like the sample portable machine Serial No. 6679 furnished to the General Company unless by mutual agreement improvements are adopted.

If any failure to comply with such warranty, excepting damage in transit, neglect, abuse or improper use of such machines, appears within one (1) year from the date of shipment, the Standard Company upon receipt of such machine or machines or parts thereof delivered prepaid at the Standard Sewing Machine Company factory in Cleveland, Ohio, will repair or replace such

Contract Page 4

59

Like the later **FREDERICK OSANN** Company and all the **OSANN** Corporation **(SINGER)** *Sewhandy* machines, the GE *MODEL A* machines produced after mid 1932 had cast iron beds that increased their weight to 15¾ pounds. Some of the 11 ¾ pounds GE *MODEL A*s with aluminum beds should still exist, but they will be rare. Note: If a magnet sticks to yours, it is a cast iron *Model A.* For more on the GE Model A, see page 127.

Osann Corporation (SINGER) Sewhandy

SINGER SEWING MACHINE COMPANY

The **SINGER** Sewing Machine Company has a rich and varied history. However, it was not always on friendly terms with its competitors. Numerous legal disagreements (including possible patent infringement) are recorded in its history. It was for a long time beginning in 1853 the dominant sewing machine manufacture in the world.

SINGER had its own design works and had its own portable sewing machine designs. The **SINGER** Company filed for a US patent on a portable sewing machine before 1920, and introduced the **SINGER** "portable electric" 99K for sale to the public in 1921. It was basically a hand-crank with a motor attached.

SEW WHEREVER YOU WISH

You will never know how convenient a modern sewing machine can be until you use a Singer Portable Electric. For here is a machine so compact that you can pick it up, carry it, sew with it wherever you wish! And when sewing time is done, your Singer is placed in a closet — out of sight and out of the way.

Only in a genuine Singer do you obtain enduring Singer quality and perfect workmanship. Hidden power under perfect control does all the work. No need even for an extra light—the Singerlight attached to the machine casts its soft rays upon your work, shielding your eyes from glare.

Singer Sewing Machine Co.
INCORPORATED

206 W. Clark St.   Phone 3044

May we give you an interesting demonstration?

SINGER ad from that time

SINGER faced the same design problem that the other manufacturers had. The typical electric portable of the 1920's was heavy with a carrying weight of over 30 pounds. They may have been called "portable," but you would not want to have to "port" them very far. They needed a lightweight design. One of their earlier designs (SINGER 100) that looks similar to a FEATHERWEIGHT (without the hinged table) is shown below:

US Patent Records show that the original Sewhandy inventor, Richard K. Holmann, was working with SINGER in 1931 on sewing machine designs. And in late 1933, SINGER introduced its FEATHERWEIGHT to the sewing world at the Chicago World's Fair.

Whether the *Sewhandy* was too much competition for the FEATHERWEIGHT, or their maybe patent or design infringement problems, or possibly Frederick Osann just wanted to sell is not recorded. How and why the Frederick Osann Company sold the rights remain unknown.

For whatever reason(s), in mid 1934 the Frederick Osann Company was sold to the SINGER Manufacturing Company for an undisclosed amount. SINGER immediately formed a second corporation called the OSANN Corporation (not the Frederick Osann Company) to continue manufacturing the STANDARD sewing machine product line including the *Sewhandy*.

None of the other Frederick Osann Sewing Machines appear to have been produced later by SINGER and the SINGER website does not mention any acquisition of the Frederick Osann Company. However, the records do show that SINGER continued manufacturing the long gone "STANDARD Sewing Machine of Cleveland" line along with the *Sewhandy* well into 1938.

THE OSANN CORPORATION
SINGER

The OSANN Corporation was formed by SINGER to continue the sewing machine manufacturing business of the former Frederick Osann Company. Osann offices were established in Elizabeth New Jersey to be near the SINGER manufacturing plant. It would appear that for some time, FEATHERWEIGHTs and *Sewhandys* were manufactured by SINGER on production lines in the same plant.

The OSANN Corporation Sewhandy is similar to those models that came before it. The easiest way to tell if you have an OSANN -SINGER *Sewhandy* made from mid 1934 to the end of production in late 1938 is to look for the label on the front bed edge. An OSANN - SINGER *Sewhandy* will have the decal reading:

You can also recognize an OSANN – SINGER model by looking at the motor or motor plate. Machines made prior to SINGER taking over used the **GENERAL ELECTRIC** motor. As soon as **SINGER** formed their **OSANN** Corporation, they mounted a **OSANN** Corporation label plate over an unlabeled **SINGER BRK/BUK** series motor. See the example below. For more on this model, see page 137.

It does not appear that **SINGER** continued the exclusive marketing contract for the **GENERAL ELECTRIC** *MODEL A*, and for some period of time in 1934 thru 1935 both models (with different motors) may have been marketed under different labels at the same time. GE Model A's seem to have disappeared from the retail scene by mid 1935.

The records do show that **SINGER** continued using the "STANDARD Sewing Machine of Cleveland" name, and manufactured the

STANDARD product line (including the *Sewhandy* under the successors to STANDARD label) until November 1938 (more than nine years after the original STANDARD had failed).

So on November 18, 1938, SINGER dissolved the OSANN Corporation and all production ended of the sewing machine known as the

Sewhandy.

HOLMANN & OSANN

You may wonder what happened to the original *Sewhandy* sewing machine designer Richard Holmann (Hohmann) and the *Sewhandy* manufacturer Frederick Osann. Interestingly, in 1939, US Patent records show Richard Holmann (Hohmann) and Frederick Osann working together again. As co-inventors on four sewing machine patents (US Patents 2247381, 2247379, 2247382, and 2247383). One of the patents was assigned to the White Sewing Machine Corp, while the other three were

assigned to Sears & Roebuck for their in house sewing machine line.

More *Sewhandy* PATENTS

Actual improvements to the *Sewhandy* came to a halt when SINGER (OSANN CORPORATION) acquired it. Even so, US Patents applications continued using the *Sewhandy* design.

US Patent 2,056,125

Sept. 29, 1936.   R. L. PLUMLEY ET AL   2,056,125

HAND OPERATED ATTACHMENT FOR SEWING MACHINES

Filed May 15, 1935   2 Sheets-Sheet 1

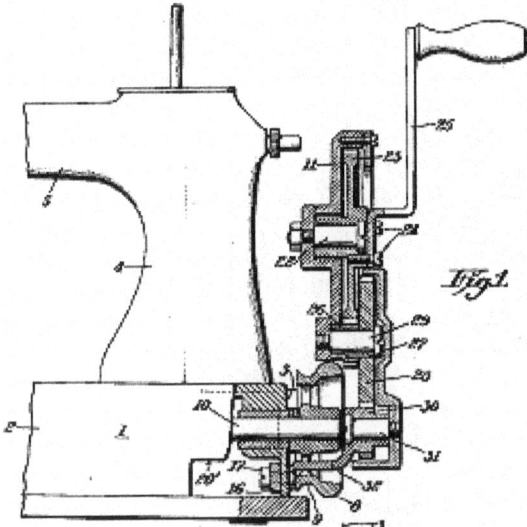

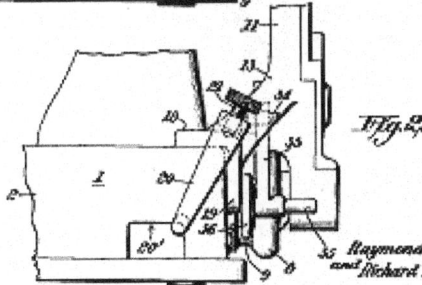

Fig.1

Fig.2

Inventor
Raymond L. Plumley
and Richard K. Hohmann

Witness: By   Henry J. Miller   Attorney

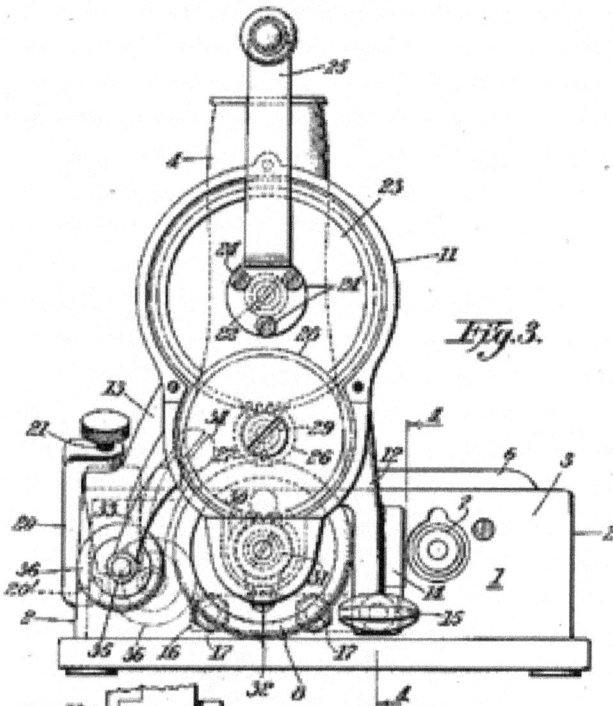

Fig.3.

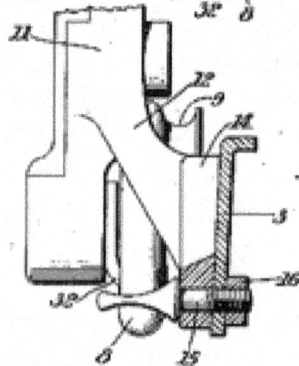

Fig.4.

Inventor
Raymond L. Plumley
and Richard K. Hohmann

Witness
By

Attorney

70

US Patent 2,217,895

Oct. 15, 1940.   G. A. FLECKENSTEIN   2,217,895

SEWING MACHINE

Filed Sept. 28, 1939   4 Sheets-Sheet 1

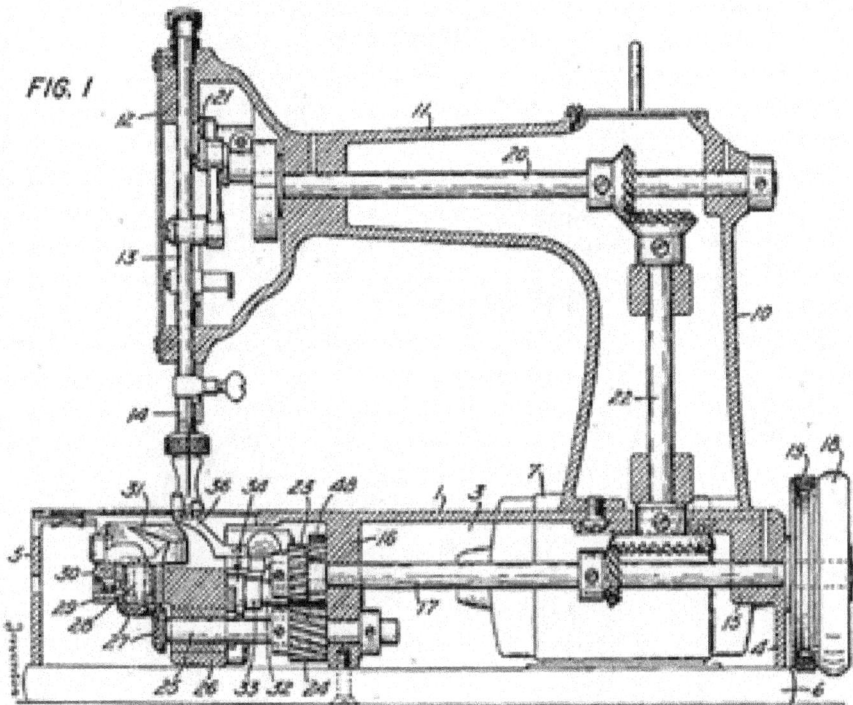

FIG. 1

George A. Fleckenstein

By Henry J. Miller
Attorney

71

US Patent 2,247,381

July 1, 1941.　　　R. K. HOHMANN ET AL　　　2,247,381

SEWING MACHINE DRIVE MEANS

Original Filed Dec. 29, 1939

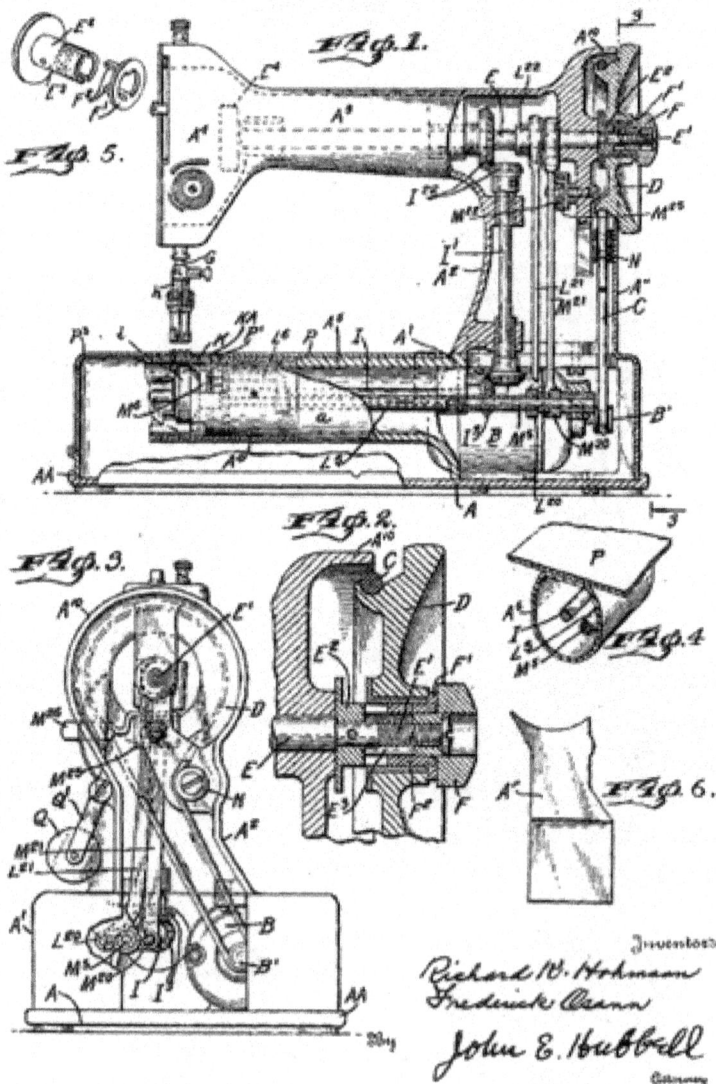

Fig. 1.

Fig. 5.

Fig. 2.

Fig. 3.

Fig. 4.

Fig. 6.

Inventors
Richard W. Hohmann
Frederick Osann
John E. Hubbell
Attorney

72

US Patent 2,276,246

March 10, 1942.   G. A. FLECKENSTEIN   2,276,246

SEWING MACHINE

Filed Oct. 24, 1939   4 Sheets-Sheet 1

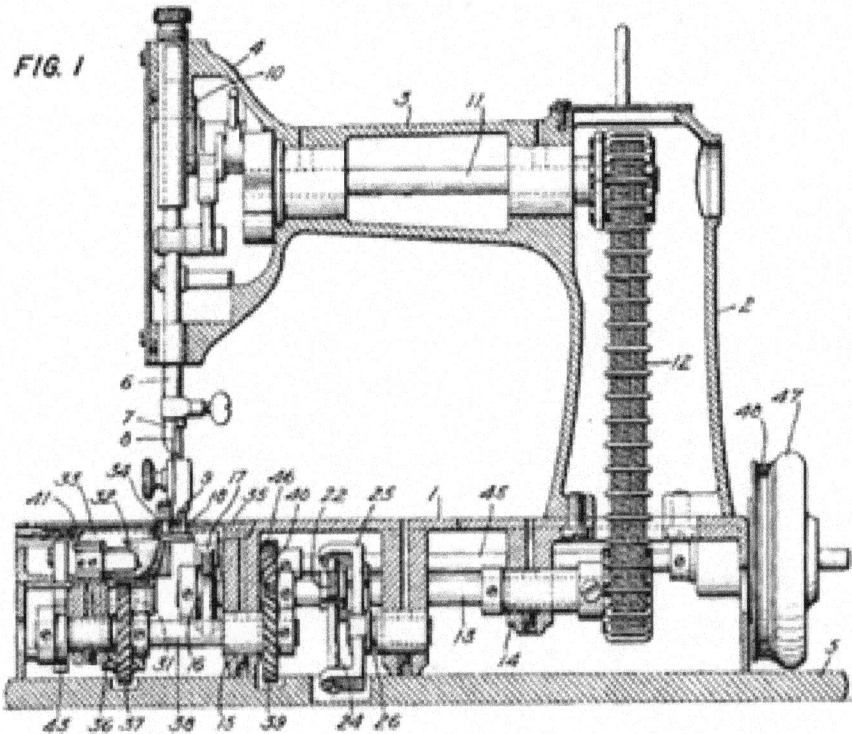

FIG. I

Inventor

GEORGE A. FLECKENSTEIN

By Henry J Miller

Attorney

Sewhandy ADVERTISING

Newspapers and magazines made, and still make, a lot of their money from running advertisements. Lucky for us....for if it had not been profitable, these ads would not exist. These old newspaper and magazine issues give us informative and enjoyable snapshots of what went on in the past. While it was not their intent, the publishers have preserved a very rich source of information for later generations

This chapter is a collection of *Sewhandy* and GE Model-A ads that ran in newspapers across the United States. Some of the ads are extremely detailed. Others are no more than the very simple classified ads. I have included even the simple ones because they illustrate the selling price in a particular month and year. Many of these ads ran on different dates, and the listed date is just one of those publication dates.

I found both the ad designs and prices very interesting. I hope you have as much fun as I did taking the trip back down memory lane. Enjoy.

If you do enjoy old sewing machine ads, you might also look at my other book, "*the Featherweight Ads*" that illustrates 80 SINGER Model 221 Featherweight ads.

A few famous quotes about advertising...

"The most truthful part of a newspaper is the advertisements."
~Thomas Jefferson

"Advertising says to people, 'Here's what we've got. Here's what it will do for you. Here's how to get it."
~Leo Burnett

"Advertising is the greatest art form of the 20th century."
~Leo Burnett

"Advertising is the genie which is transforming America into a place of comfort, luxury and ease for millions."
~William Allen White

A TINY MOTOR
Does All the Work!

Come! Sit down and sew with this electric sewing machine. See how free both hands are — both feet at ease. A touch on the speed control and the stitching flows swiftly along as you guide it.

With the Sewhandy electric sewing machine it is easy to make charming frocks with a truly *professional* air. Snap on an attachment and you can plait, ruffle or shir as easily as you seam. You work with effortless ease — restful comfort — sheer *enjoyment in sewing*.

The Sewhandy machines are portable and come in four different colors with a black or tan carrying case.

May 15, 1929

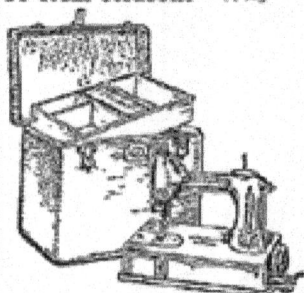

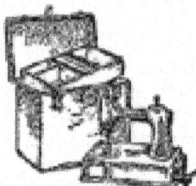

For the Beloved One who heads your List—why not a Modern Power-Driven Sewing Machine?

The New *Sewhandy*
Electric Portable
Sewing Machine

Use it on your Card Table
Does not vibrate

Here's a portable Sewing Machine that weighs only 12 pounds, and does everything a big machine does: It's a non-clogging Rotary, with General Electric Motor.

$20 Will Be Allowed You for Your Old Sewing Machine

And we need not call for the old one until after Christmas. Enabling you to make your gift a complete surprise.

Sale on Terms as Low as $5.00 Down and $5.00 a Month

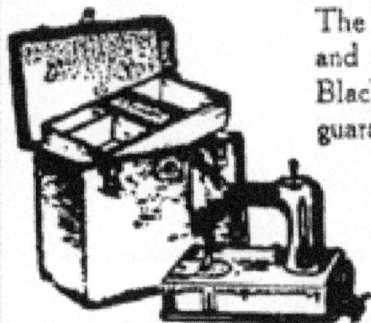

The Machine comes in Green, Blue, Rose and Black—in a carrying Case of Tan or Black — All attachments — Lessons Free — guaranteed for life.

October 23, 1929

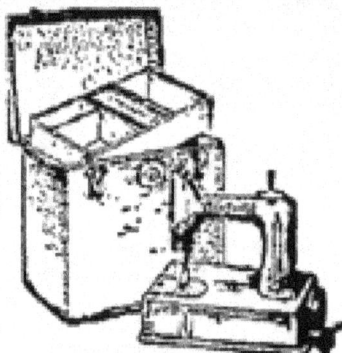

SEWING MACHINES

Never before have women taken such an interest in sewing or enjoyed such comforts as they are now able to do.

Sewhandy Portable Electric

This Machine Only Weighs 12 Pounds.

It is a full Rotary and will not Vibrate.

Can be used on your ordinary Card Table.

Any room in your home can be a sewing room.

Phone us for a demonstration in your own home.

Four colors to choose from.

Green, Blue, Rose and Black.

Sewhandy

December 13, 1929

Sewhandy Electrical Sewing Machine

Made and Guaranteed by the Standard Sewing Machine Co.

Weighs only 12 pounds, fits in convenient carrying case. Does not vibrate, can be used on a card table. Has sewlight and all attachments. Sews the sheerest and heaviest materials.

$20.00 allowance on your old machine

April 22, 1930

Sewing Machines

All New Machines

Standard makes, and guaranteed for 10 years. Domestic Rotary Electric, Standard Rotary Electric, Sewhandy Portable Electric, Domestic Desk Electric. Regularly $105... **$52.50**

Domestic Electric.
Regularly $99.50 .... **$49.75**

Standard Table Model—Regularly
$99.50 .... **$49.75**

Standard Desk Model —Regularly
$110 .... **$55**

Sewhandy Portable Electric.
Regularly
$87.50 .... **$43.75**

$5 Down, Balance Monthly

January 28, 1932

Sewing Machines at Half Price

"Standard"

Regularly $99.50, for............$50
Regularly $105, for $50

"Sewhandy" Portable

Regularly $87.50, for........$39.95

"Domestic"

Regular $105 Model $52.50
Regular $95 Model $49.50
Regular $99.50 Model $49.75

Third Floor, Electric Appliances

February 2, 1932

You Must See This Perfect Little Jewel

General Electric Sewing Machine

Really
Portable
15½ Pounds

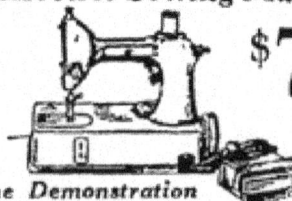

$76.⁵⁰

Use Our Easy Payment Plan

Ask for a Home Demonstration

Really something radically new in an all-electric really portable sewing machine. You must see it SEW... anything or everything...without adjustment. SWIFT ...VIBRATIONLESS. First Floor.

CAPWELL-SULLIVAN & FURTH

April 19, 1932

More Clothes CHEAPER
with a

G. E. Sewing Machine

$5.00 Down - $1.25 Weekly

If you want lots of nice clothes, you can have them by making them yourself.

A General Electric Portable Sewing Machine will enable you to make them quickly — besides it is truly portable. Weighs only 15 3-4 pounds. Call us for a demonstration.

July 18, 1932

$500 in Gifts FREE!

NOTHING TO BUY!

THIS IS WHAT WE SHALL GIVE AWAY!

General Electric Sewing Machine . . .
14-Cup Coffee Urn Set . . .
$30 Telechron Electric Clock . . .
Latest Style Bridge Lamp . . .
Floor Lamps, Percolators, Boudoir Lamps
and many other valuable gifts.

TODAY AND TOMORROW

Come In for Your Ticket
10 A. M. to 10 P. M.
Some of the Gifts will be given away
Tonight, starting at 7:30.

Authorized
GENERAL ELECTRIC
HOME APPLIANCE DEALER

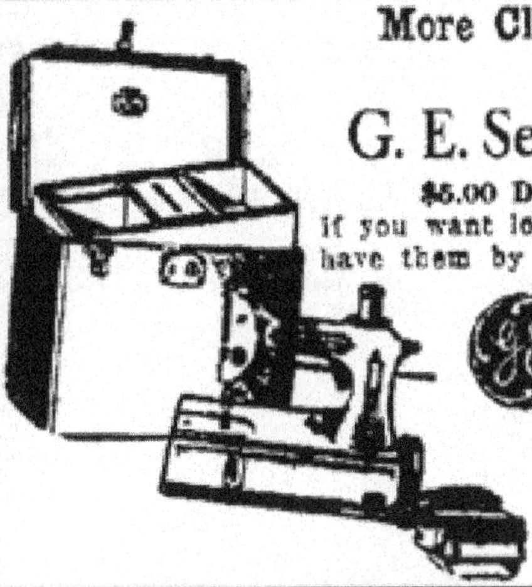

October 7, 1932

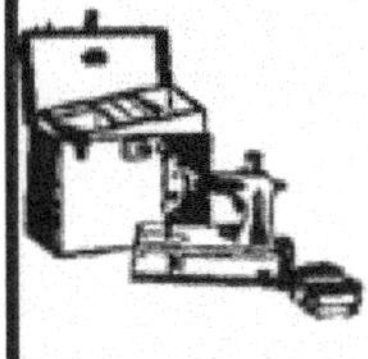

A NEW General Electric portable sewing machine for only $49.75. Terms if desired. Kelly & Zimmerman, Your General Electric Dealer.

April 3, 1935

Sewhandy BROCHURES

These are examples of the brochures that came along with the *Sewhandy* machines.

1929 STANDARD SEWING MACHINE COMPANY
of Cleveland Guarantee Certificate

SO LIGHT
SO COMPACT
SO USEFUL

Sewhandy

A "STANDARD"
PORTABLE ELECTRIC

1935 *Sewhandy* - Page 1

USE IT
ANY PLACE

Upstairs in your room—down-
stairs with the family—on the
porch on warm days—sew any-
place with the "Sewhandy".

Easy to operate

1935 *Sewhandy* - Page 2

WEIGHS ONLY 15½ POUNDS —
THE FIRST TRULY PORTABLE MACHINE

Trouble free

1935 *Sewhandy* **- Page 3**

TAKE IT ANY PLACE

Off to a friend's home—away on a vacation — traveling — you can carry the "Sewhandy" as easily as an overnight bag.

Easy to carry...

1935 *Sewhandy* - Page 4

THE ADVANTAGES OF HAVING A

Sewhandy

IN YOUR HOME

*T*HE making of attractive dresses is just one of the hundred-and-one uses of a "Sewhandy." Many women consider it a wise investment for use only in remodeling, altering and mending. Others find that curtains, draperies, slipcovers, bedspreads, luncheon sets and other articles for the home may be made at great savings. When there are children in the family it is so much fun to make up attractive clothes for them. Almost every day finds a new use for your "Sewhandy." The "Sewhandy" has the added advantages of lightness and compactness. It may be carried with ease to any part of the house, placed on any light card table, and it is ready to serve you.

1932 *Sewhandy*

THE SECRET OF Charm

October 1932 GE Model A - Page 1

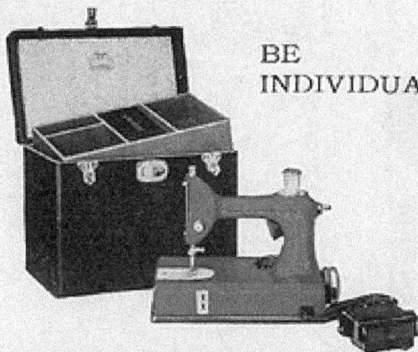

BE INDIVIDUAL...

MAKE YOUR OWN CLOTHES

OF COURSE the secret of charm lies in being well groomed! Every woman knows that! Good-looking clothes are worth their weight in gold and every woman can have them now at an amazingly low cost . . . . There's no surer way or no quicker way than to make them with a G-E Portable Sewing Machine.

It is light . . . . lighter than any other sewing machine—in fact it is the only actually Portable Sewing Machine on the market . . . . It does not vibrate! You can use it any place . . . . its rotary bobbin and open hook mechanism eliminate that most undesirable feature of the ordinary sewing machine . . . . clogging . . . . You can sew the daintiest materials and even 3-ply overcoat cloth with no adjustment to the machine! And you can make a complete wardrobe quicker, easier and at a saving you never dreamed possible! Come in and see it! Seeing is believing!

GENERAL ELECTRIC
PORTABLE SEWING MACHINE

October 1932 GE Model A - Page 2

A card table makes
a good work table.
(Right)

Carry it easily to
any room in the
house. (Below)

A good looking piece of
luggage in its carrying
case. The case may also be
used as an overnight bag.
(Right)

October 1932 GE Model A - Page 3

Sewhandy

STANDARD SEWING MACHINE COMPANY • CLEVELAND • U.S.A.

for your home

THE SEWHANDY is an innovation—an entirely different sewing machine that is very alluring to the woman of today who likes to give expression to her own tastes in creating what she wears. Its convenient size, its weight of less than twelve pounds, and its ability to do everything you can ask of it, not only better but more quickly than any other sewing machine, places it in a unique position.

By adapting the materials and patterns of your selection to your individual style, through the assistance of our Color and Fitting Advisory Service, and then working at home with the help of your SEWHANDY, you can vastly improve the personality and modishness of your wardrobe, and do it with no exertion and at far less cost than would be possible through the most careful selection of ready mades.

Your SEWHANDY may be finished in beautiful marine blue, as shown on the opposite page; or you may choose larch green or ashes of roses if better suited to your needs.

1930 *Sewhandy* - Page 1

SEW IN THE SUNLIGHT

Your SEWHANDY and a card table are all you need to do your sewing in the sunny room at any hour of the day. Take it where you will be convenient to the telephone, or to respond to the doorbell. It is easily carried in one hand and needs only access to an electric outlet or socket. It gives you the freedom of your house while sewing.

And so practical it is, that you can stitch the daintiest materials, or heaviest woolens with no adjustment to the machine. You can bind a whole apron in a few brief moments.

REASONS WHY YOU WILL LIKE THE SEWHANDY

1. The Sewhandy weighs less than 12 pounds, including motor, and but nineteen in its washable leatherette case.
2. Always under control, the Sewhandy can be operated so slowly that you can watch every stitch, or it can be speeded up faster than any other sewing machine.
3. The Sewhandy will automatically feed georgette or chiffon without puckering. You need not use paper backing to assure a flat seam.
4. Gear driven throughout, and with all rotary motion, the Sewhandy is practically vibrationless. It will not "walk" on the lightest table, even at top speed.
5. The Sewhandy will not clog. Its improved round bobbin and open hook mechanism eliminate this most undesirable feature of many sewing machines.

1930 *Sewhandy* - Page 2

Hemming, pleating and tucking, too, are made easier and swifter under its magic touch. No wonder the SEWHANDY is loved by modern women.

Created by sewing machine experts who realized that women want a really portable sewing machine that would do even more than any other sewing machine made, the SEWHANDY combines beauty of form, color and small size with the utmost in practicability. Simplicity of design, elimination of vibration, even at highest speed, an even stitch on both sides of the material, are only a few of the outstanding features that have been embodied in the SEWHANDY.

6. Its General Electric motor assures the Sewhandy of freedom from electrical troubles.
7. With motor and all parts hidden in the base and arm of the machine, you have the utmost in cleanliness, with no danger of getting oil spots or machine dirt on your material.
8. With marine blue, larch green, or ashes of roses from which to select, you can have a machine that will attractively blend with your home decorations.
9. The Sewhandy sewlite throws a clear light just where you need it for sewing ease.
10. The attractive case of washable leatherette material measures only 13 inches its longest way and makes an attractive piece of luggage. It may be tucked into the tonneau of your car, and stored on your closet shelf when not in use.

1930 *Sewhandy* - Page 3

Sewhandy

STANDARD SEWING MACHINE COMPANY · CLEVELAND · USA

REG. U.S. PAT. OFF.

is now on display here. Ask the demonstrator to tell
you about it.

FREDERICK OSANN COMPANY
245 SEVENTH AVENUE
NEW YORK CITY
WATKINS 7596

1930 *Sewhandy* - Page 4

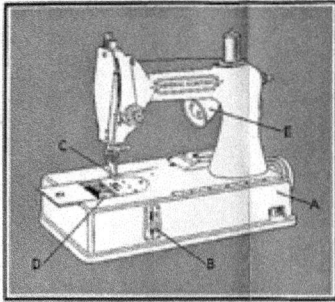

THE NEW G-E
PORTABLE SEWING MACHINE

SIMPLE IN CONSTRUCTION

No Complicated Parts

A It is vibrationless . . . . gear driven . . . . motor and hand wheel in the base . . . . low center of gravity.

B Convenient stitch regulator . . . . machine may be regulated while in motion.

C 15 x 1 type needle . . . . can be purchased anywhere . . . . cannot be inserted incorrectly.

D No clogging . . . . prevented by open end hook and free floating bobbin.

E Convenient spot-light using standard type lamp.

From the
SHEEREST
OF SILKS...

To the
HEAVIEST OF
WOOLENS..

WITHOUT
ADJUSTMENT

USE IT ON ANY

1932 GE Model A

1929 *Sewhandy*

The *Sewhandy*
is made in a
variety of
charming colors
as illustrated

Marine Blue

Larch Green

The Machine
itself with G. E.
Electric Motor

*Weighs Only
12 Pounds!*

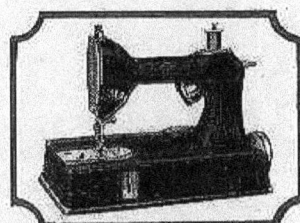

French Maroon

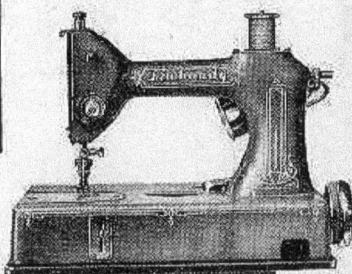

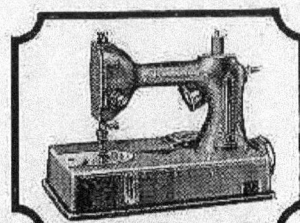

Velvet Black

"*Portable Without a Porter*"

1929 *Sewhandy*

At first
you'll admire—
then soon you'll
acquire
The

Sewhandy

1929 *Sewhandy*

**1936 OSANN CORPORATION
SINGER *Sewhandy***

IDENTIFYING YOUR
Sewhandy

The *Sewhandy* (including **GENERAL ELECTRIC** *MODEL A*) was produced from February 1928 thru late 1938. It evolved and went thru numerous changes during its 10-year manufacturing run.

Some of the changes were extensive, but most of them were minor details such as labeling. Those changes allow us to estimate an approximate manufacturing date for each machine.

I have been unable to find a manufacturers listing of what serial number was assigned on what date. There were four different companies (Standard Sewing Machine Company of Cleveland, Frederick Osann Company of New York, The Osann Corporation Singer, and General Electric) involved in the manufacturing or marketing, and it appears that each had different serial numbers.

In this chapter, I will identify specific details on a *Sewhandy* for each period of time. If your machine has that feature, then it will fall into that period of time.

One exception.... The Face Plates were sometimes switched (just like on the **SINGER** 221) depending on owner preferences.

Place the front of the machine facing you. Look at the area of the machine bed top directly in front of the bottom of the vertical arm. Refer to the photos below.

Does your machine have the decal in front of the bottom of the arm in gold lettering?

DES. PAT. 80185
OTHER PATS. PENDING

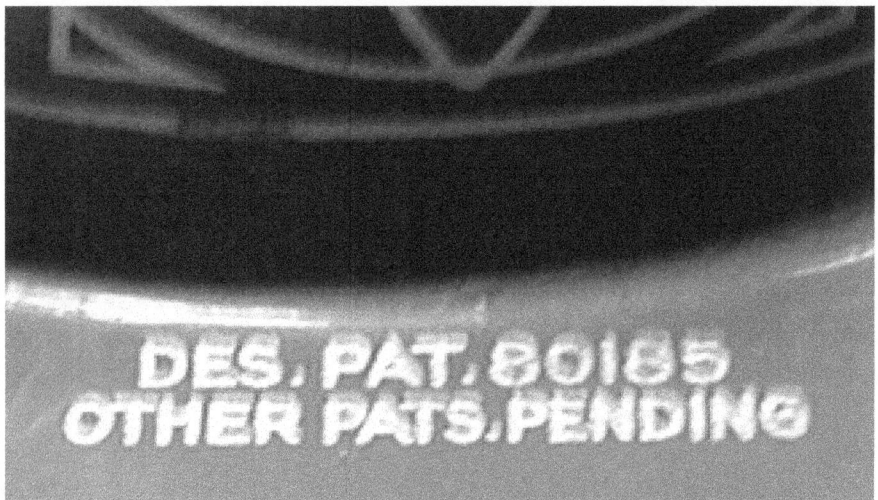

U. S. Design Patent 80185 was granted on December 29, 1929. *Sewhandy* machines made after this date, and all GE *MODEL A's*, had this decal.

If your machine has this decal and it is a *Sewhandy*, go to page 119.

If your machine has this decal and it is a General Electric *Model A*, go to page 127.

If your machine does not have the DES. PAT. 80185 OTHER PATS. PENDING decal, it was made by prior to December 29, 1929. Continue on to page 109.

**STANDARD Sewing machine of
Cleveland *Sewhandy***

STANDARD *Sewhandy*

There are three variants of the STANDARD *Sewhandy*. The models break-down into the following groups:

1) STANDARD (Early) produced from the earliest production beginning in February thru August 1928.

2) *Sewhandy* (Mid) manufactured from August 1928 thru early 1929.

3) STANDARD *Sewhandy* (Late) made from early 1929 thru mid 1929.

All three variants share the same design features, with a few exceptions. These exceptions date the machine. All three share the following:

1) The machines have aluminum beds weighing 11¾ pounds.

2) They come in four colors: Green, Blue, Rose, and Black.

3) There is a winged STANDARD Sewing Machine Company logo in the center of the machine bed. There are two versions of the logo.

Early Decal (Cleveland, U.S.A. below logo)

Later Decal (Cleveland U.S.A. above logo)

4) The Slide Plate has a round hole.

5) This *Sewhandy* has a GE motor.

6) The Face Plate is plain chrome.

7) The serial number is on the right side of the Stitch Regulator Plate (starts with a "J-").

8) All have the General Electric 75 Watt Lamp Shade and Socket Assembly with the long chrome end.

On this unit, the brown switch has "GE" molded into the surface.

Which STANDARD do you have? Place the front of the machine facing you. Look at the neck of your *Sewhandy* and match the gold lettered decal with the one of the pictures on the following pages.

Earliest Production

The neck decal design below is found on **STANDARD** Sewing Machine of Cleveland machines from the earliest production from February thru August 1928. If yours reads *"Sewhandy"*, move on to "Mid Production" on the next page.

The earliest winged logos have "Cleveland, U.S.A." below the wings. These are on the **STANDARD** Sewing Machine of Cleveland machines from the earliest production from March thru August 1928. If yours has "Cleveland U.S.A." above the wings, move on to "Mid Production".

Mid Production

The neck decal design below is found on a STANDARD Sewing Machine of Cleveland *Sewhandy* from August 1928 thru early 1929. If yours reads "STANDARD *Sewhandy*", move on to "Late Production" below.

The Mid and Late Production logo on the bed is the same. It has Cleveland U.S.A. above the wings and is shown below.

Late Production

The neck decal design below is found on a STANDARD Sewing Machine of Cleveland machine from early to mid 1929. Note: If your *Sewhandy* has "STANDARD *Sewhandy*" with no bordering decal around it, then you have a later OSANN Corp SINGER version with a cast iron bed. Go to page 137.

Remember, all of the STANDARD *Sewhandy* sewing machines had aluminum beds with cast iron arms. If a magnet sticks to your bed, it is NOT a *Sewhandy* machine made by the STANDARD Sewing Machine Company, but is a later model from either the FREDERICK OSANN Company on page 119, or the OSANN Corp SINGER on page 137.

Note: It is not possible to tell where the last STANDARD *Sewhandy* model stops and the first FREDERICK OSANN Company *Sewhandy* begins. All we know is that it was sometime in mid 1929. This is when FREDERICK OSANN acquired and became President of the STANDARD Sewing Machine Company of Cleveland.

The original carrying case for all these models had two brass Eagle Lock of Terryville, Conn outer latches with a brass SOSY of New York center key latch marked "made in Germany" and "Pat Pending."

FREDERICK OSANN Company
Sewhandy

FREDERICK OSANN Company
Sewhandy

The next *Sewhandy* machines are those manufactured by the FREDERICK OSANN Company, a corporation of New York. Do not confuse this with the later OSANN Corporation - SINGER, a corporation of Pennsylvania.

These *Sewhandy* sewing machines were manufactured from mid 1929 until early 1932. Note: As written previously, it is not possible to tell where the last STANDARD *Sewhandy* model stops and the first FREDERICK OSANN Company *Sewhandy* begins.

Because of the marketing and distribution agreement with GE in June 1931, *Sewhandy* marketing ceased. All of the production beginning in early 1932 was labeled "GENERAL ELECTRIC (GE) *MODEL* A". This continued until SINGER acquired the FREDERICK OSANN Company in 1934.

The FREDERICK OSANN Company *Sewhandy* machines also had aluminum beds weighing 11 ¾ pounds.

Other details follow:

3) The machines came in four colors: Marine Blue, Larch Green, French Maroon, and Velvet Black.

4) There is a **STANDARD** Sewing Machine Company logo with Cleveland U.S.A. above the wings in the center of the machine bed.

5) The neck decal design below is found on all **FREDERICK OSANN** Company Sewhandy machines. Note: If your *Sewhandy* has "**STANDARD** *Sewhandy*" with no bordering decal around it, then you have a later OSANN Corp-SINGER version with a cast iron bed. Go to page 137.

6) All but the earliest of this model has the DES. PAT. 80185 decal.

7) The Slide Plate has a round hole.

8) The early Face Plate is plain chrome. This is the same one that is used on the earlier STANDARD *Sewhandy* sewing machines.

9) The later models have the ornate floral urn scroll design on their Face Plate.

10) The serial number is on the right side of the Stitch Regulator Plate (starts with a "J-").

11) This *Sewhandy* also has the GE motor.

If your *Sewhandy* does not have the GENERAL ELECTRIC motor, but has an OSANN CORP motor, go to page 137.

12) All have the General Electric 75 Watt Lamp Shade and Socket Assembly with the long chrome end.

On this unit, the brown switch has "GE" molded into the surface.

GENERAL ELECTRIC *MODEL A*

GENERAL ELECTRIC
MODEL A

The next *Sewhandy* machines are those distributed and sold by GENERAL ELECTRIC (GE). These machines were not labeled as *Sewhandy* machines, but were identified as the GENERAL ELECTRIC *MODEL A*. (Sewhandy production stopped in early 1932).

The *MODEL A*s were manufactured for GE from July 1931 until mid 1934 by the FREDERICK OSANN Corporation at the STANDARD Sewing Machine Company of Cleveland factory.

In mid 1934, SINGER bought out the FREDERICK OSANN Company, and subsequently formed a dummy corporation, the OSANN Corporation, to continue manufacturing the STANDARD Sewing Machine product line. From mid 1934 on for a couple of years, the OSANN Corporation SINGER manufactured the *MODEL A* for GE.

Like the later FREDERICK OSANN Company and all the OSANN Corporation (SINGER) *Sewhandy* machines, the GE *MODEL A* machines produced after mid 1932 had cast iron beds that increased their weight to 15¾ pounds. Some of the 11 ¾ pounds GE *MODEL A*s with aluminum beds should still exist, but they will be rare. Note: If a magnet sticks to yours, it is a cast iron *Model A.*

Other details follow:
   1) *MODEL A*s came in one color: Green.

2) The neck decal design below is found on all the **GENERAL ELECTRIC** *MODEL A* machines.

3) There is a GE logo in the center of the machine bed on the early *MODEL A*s, but the logo is gone on the later ones.

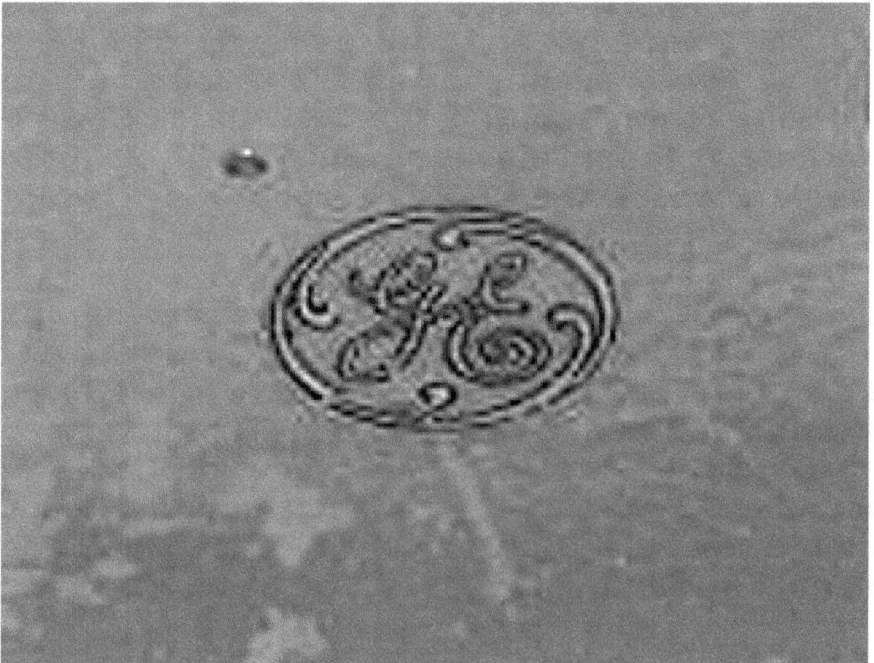

4) The DES. PAT. 80185 decal is on all GE MODEL A machines.

5) The Slide Plate has a round hole on the early models.

6) On the later *MODEL A* machines, the Slide Plate has a grooved indent finger pull instead of a hole to pull it open.

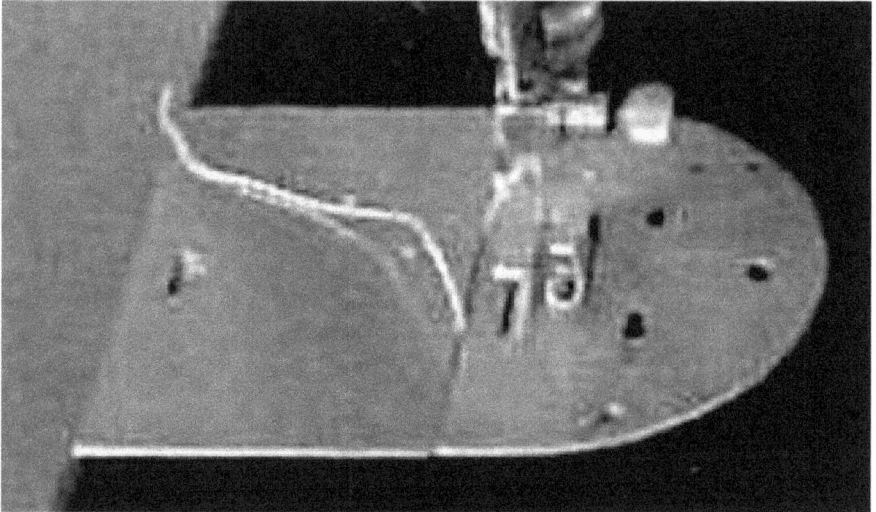

7) The *MODEL A* has a GE motor.

SEWING MACHINE MOTOR
MODEL NO.
WHEN ORDERING PARTS GIVE MODEL NO.
VOLTS 110 CYC.
NO.
GENERAL ELECTRIC CO.
SCHENECTADY, N.Y. U.S.A.

8) The Face Plate on the early *MODEL A* has the ornate floral urn scroll design.

9) The later models have the GE design on their Face Plate.

10) The serial number on the earlier *MODEL A* is on a plate on the rear of the machine. See the photo below.

11) The serial number on the later *MODEL A* is on a plate in the bobbin access well. See the photo below.

12) All have the General Electric 75-Watt Lamp Shade and Socket Assembly with the short chrome end. Compare this with the long chrome end on pages 113 and 125.

13) On this model, the brown switch has no markings. Compare this with the "GE" marked switch on page 113 and 125.

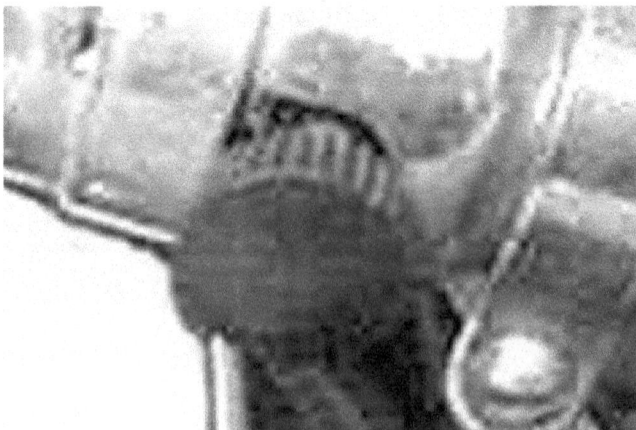

14) The *MODEL A* also has a 6 inch ruler decal on the front bed edge. This decal is unique to the **GENERAL ELECTRIC** *MODEL A.*

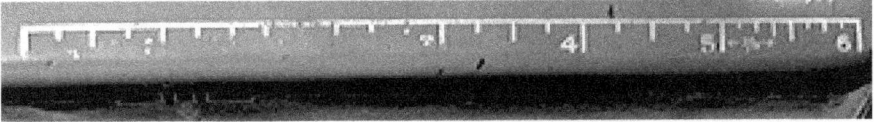

15) The *MODEL A* Stitch Regulator Plate does not have a Serial Number on it. Instead, it has the words "SHORT" – "STITCH" – "LONG" printed on its right side.

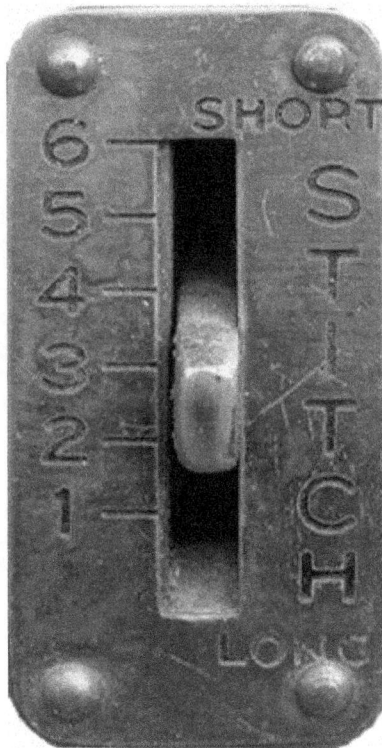

OSANN Corporation-SINGER
Sewhandy

OSANN Corporation-SINGER *Sewhandy*

These are the newest of the *Sewhandy* machines. They were manufactured from mid 1934 until late 1938.

In mid 1934, SINGER bought out the FREDERICK OSANN Company and subsequently formed their dummy corporation, the OSANN Corporation, to continue manufacturing the *Sewhandy* machines along with the rest of the STANDARD Sewing Machine product line.

The OSANN Corporation – SINGER *Sewhandy* machines all have the cast iron beds making these models weigh 15¾ pounds. These models came in one color: Black.

The easiest way to tell if you have an OSAAN - SINGER *Sewhandy* made from mid 1934 to the end of production in late 1938 is to look for the label on the front bed edge. An OSAAN - SINGER *Sewhandy* will have the decal reading:

**MANUFACTURED BY
THE OSANN CORPORATION
NEW YORK, N.Y.
SUCCESSORS TO**

THE STANDARD
SEWING MACHINE COMPANY

See the actual decal on the next page.

Remember, this is the OSANN Corporation that SINGER formed as their dummy corporation after they bought out the FREDERICK OSANN Company. It was based out of the SINGER headquarters in New York City with its manufacturing office in the SINGER plant at Elizabethport, NJ. This is not the FREDERICK OSANN Company that originally worked with the STANDARD Sewing Machine Company of Cleveland to produce the first *Sewhandy* machines.

You can also tell the model by looking at the motor or motor plate. Machines made prior to SINGER taking over used the GENERAL ELECTRIC motor. As soon as SINGER formed their OSANN Corporation, they mounted a OSANN Corporation label plate over an unlabeled SINGER BRK/BUK series motor. See the example on the next page.

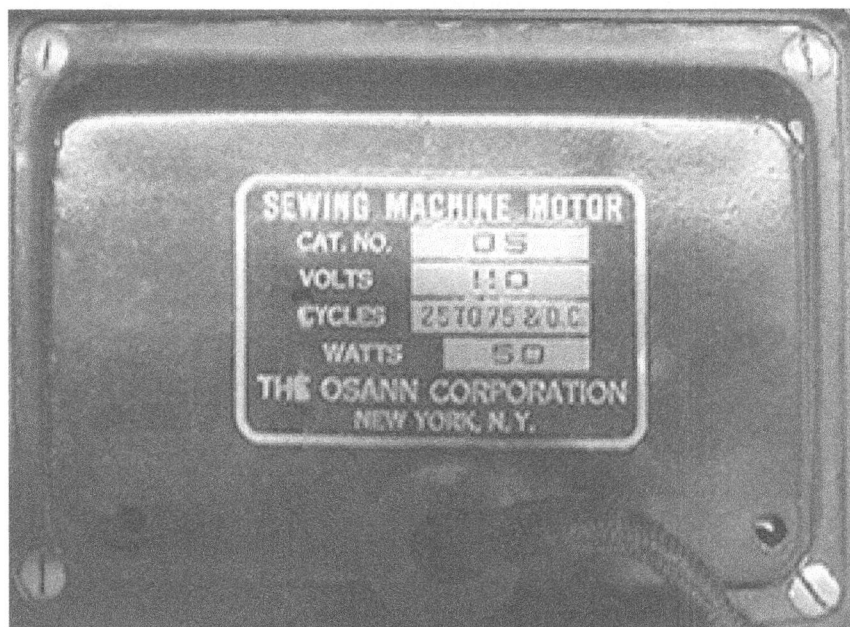

The **OSANN** Corporation – **SINGER** *Sewhandy* machine labeling or decals are much simpler. The winged **STANDARD** Sewing Machine Company logo in the center of the machine bed was eliminated.

The neck label still read Standard *Sewhandy*, but the lettering was changed and the gold borders were eliminated.

139

Other details follow:

1) **The Face Plate has the same ornate floral urn scroll design used on the FREDERICK OSANN Company** *Sewhandy***.**

16) **All have the General Electric 75 Watt Lamp Shade and Socket Assembly with the short chrome end. Compare this with the long chrome end on pages 113 and 125.**

17) **On this model, the brown switch has no markings. Compare this with the "GE" marked switch on page 13 and 125.**

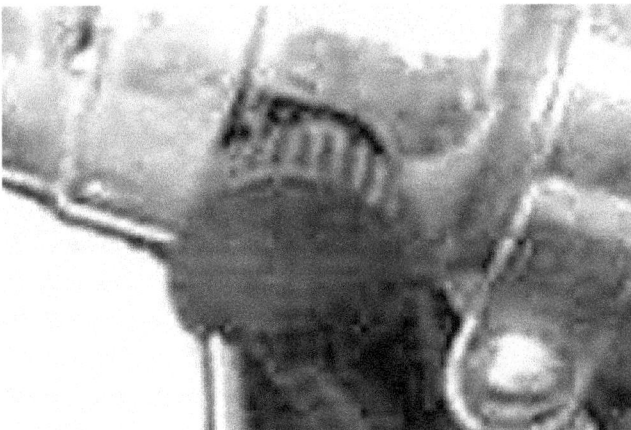

18) The Slide Plate has a grooved indent finger pull instead of a hole to pull it open.

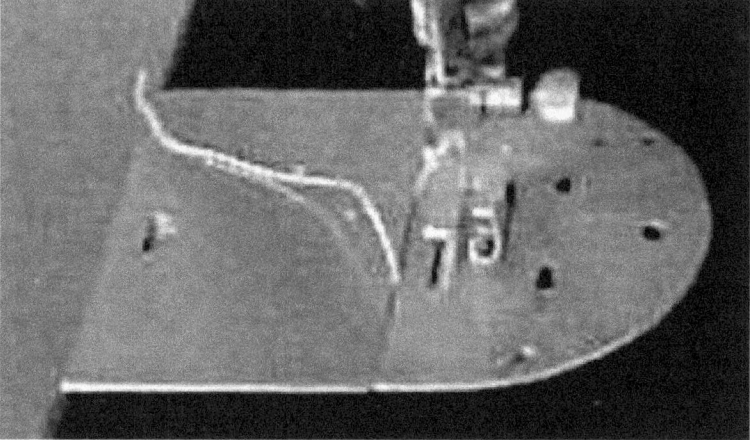

19) The serial number is on the right side of the Stitch Regulator Plate (starts with a "J-").

There are not any other differences thru the end of production in late 1938.

Model Specifications

STANDARD Sewing Machine Company *Sewhandy*

Made in Cleveland
Manufacturing Period: Feb 1928 thru Mid 1929
General Electric (GE) Motor
4 Colors: Green, Blue, Rose, and Black
Black or Tan Carrying Case
Aluminum beds making weight 11¾ lbs
Early Center Bed Decal – Cleveland USA above
Late Center Bed Decal – Cleveland USA below
Plain Chrome Face Plate
Slide Plate finger hole
No DES. PAT. 80185 on right front bed
Standard neck decal – gold borders (Early)
***Sewhandy* neck decal – gold borders (Mid)**
STANDARD *Sewhandy* neck decal – gold borders (Late)
SN on front stitch length lever plate
Long GE Lamp Shade and Socket Assembly
"GE" marking on Lamp Shade switch
Case outside latches Eagle Lock
Center latch SOSY Pat Pending

Model Specifications

FREDERICK OSANN Company
Sewhandy

Made in Cleveland
Manufacturing Period: Mid 1929 thru Early 1932
General Electric (GE) Motor
4 Colors: Larch Green, Marine Blue, French
Maroon, Velvet Black
Black or Tan Carrying Case
Aluminum beds weight 11¾ lbs
Center Bed Decal – Cleveland USA below
Plain Chrome Face Plate (Early)
Scroll Chrome Face Plate (Late)
Slide Plate finger hole
No DES. PAT. 80185 on right front bed (Earliest)
DES. PAT. 80185 on right front bed (Later)
STANDARD *Sewhandy* neck decal – gold borders
SN on front stitch length lever plate
Long GE Lamp Shade and Socket Assembly
"GE" marking on Lamp Shade switch
Case outside latches Eagle Lock
Center latch SOSY Pat Pending

Model Specifications

GENERAL ELECTRIC
MODEL A

Made in Cleveland (Early)
Made in Elizabethport, New Jersey (Later)
Manufacturing Period: July 1931 thru Mid 1934
Mid 1934 to around 1935 (SINGER)
General Electric (GE) Motor
Colors: Green
Aluminum beds 11¾ lbs to Mid 1932
Cast Iron beds 15¾ lbs after Mid 1932
"GE" Center Bed Decal (Early)
No "GE" Center Bed Decal (Late)
Scroll Chrome Face Plate (Early)
"GE" Face Plate (Late)
Slide Plate has finger groove indentation
DES. PAT. 80185 on right front bed
General Electric neck decal – no borders
STITCH on front stitch length lever plate
SN on plate in bobbin bed area (Early)
SN on rear plate below motor (Late)
6 inch rule decal on right front bed edge
Short GE Lamp Shade and Socket Assembly
No markings on Lamp Shade switch
Case outside latches Langenau Cleveland
Center latch SOSY Pat 1717930 (July 1929)

Model Specifications

OSANN Corporation SINGER
Sewhandy

Made in Elizabethport, New Jersey
Manufacturing Period: Mid 1934 thru late 1938
SINGER BRK/BUK Motor
Colors: Black
Cast Iron beds 15¾ lbs
Scroll Chrome Face Plate
Slide Plate finger groove indentation
DES. PAT. 80185 on right front bed
Standard *Sewhandy* neck decal – <u>no borders</u>
OSANN Corp "Successor" decal on front bed
SN on front stitch length lever plate
Short GE Lamp Shade and Socket Assembly
No markings on Lamp Shade switch
Case outside latches Langenau Cleveland
Center latch SOSY Pat 1717930 (July 1929)

SINGER *Sewhandy* Versus SINGER Featherweight

There has been a lot of discussion in the past about which was the "better" machine: the STANDARD/OSANN *Sewhandy* or the SINGER 221 Featherweight.

Common sense would tell you that since the *Sewhandy* design had been around since 1928, and since SINGER had access to it while designing their Model 221, that the Featherweight should be a "better" and more modern machine.

And it may have been just coincidental that SINGER introduced their re-designed Model 221 in 1935, shortly after they bought out the FREDERICK OSANN Company along with the *Sewhandy* and its patents, and created a second corporation (OSANN CORP) to manage it.

Lucky for us, SINGER continued to manufacture the now <u>OSANN SINGER *Sewhandy*</u> (with the STANDARD label) along side their 221 Featherweights in their Elizabethport factory until around 1938. This allows us to have a side-by-side comparison between a 1937 SINGER *Sewhandy* and 1937 SINGER 221 Featherweight. Note that this is a comparison of

a <u>OSANN SINGER Sewhandy</u> versus a <u>SINGER Featherweight</u>! Both machines are of about the same age and are in similar good condition.

COMPARISON

SINGER Sewhandy	Specification	SINGER 221 Featherweight
9-1/4"	Machine Height	9-1/4"
7-1/16"	Machine Width	7-1/4"
11-7/8"	Machine Length	10-1/2"
15.75 lbs	Machine Weight	11.1 lbs
5"	Mach throat width	5"
3-5/8"	Mach throat height	4"
2-3/8"	Work Space	6-1/4"
11"	Case Height	11-1/2"
8"	Case Width	8"
13"	Case Length	13"
wood/vinyl	Case construction	wood/vinyl
20.25 lbs	Case+Mach weight	16.1 lbs
AC-DC	Motor Voltage Type	AC-DC
110-120	Motor Voltage	110-120
25-75	Motor AC Cycles	25-75
66	Motor Watts	66
0.55	Motor Amp	0.55
3500	Motor RPM (Load)	3500
7800	Motor RPM (No Load)	7600
Singer	Motor Mfg	Singer
daily(A)	Oil schedule	daily(B)
18(C)	Oil Holes or points	38(D)
No Dial	Top Tension Adj.	Dial
6-20 inch	Stitch length	6-30 inch
1100	Stitches per Minute	850
Fwd	Feed Directions	Fwd-Rev

(A) oil moving parts frequently

(B) daily if continuously used; occasional if moderately used

(C) per page 5 Inst Manual - (c)1934

(D) per pages 24-26 221-1 Instructions Manual - (c)1948

Sew-off Methodology

Objective evaluations: The machines were evaluated on the following.
Machine Size
Machine Throat Width
Machine Throat Height
Carry Case + Machine Weight
Workspace to left
Motor Horsepower
Motor RPM
Power Usage
Noise
Vibration
Bobbin Size
Max Stitches per min.
Min Stitches per min.

Subjective evaluations: The machines were evaluated on the ease of sewing and working with the machines. The following tasks were considered.
Top Threading
Bobbin Loading
Bobbin Insertion
Lower Tension Adjustment
Upper Tension Adjustment
Light Coverage
Stitch Speed
Stitch Quality
Stitch Length Adjustment
Straight Stitch
Foot Pedal Operation
Overall Feel

Sew-off Conclusions

The machines are very similar in their sewing capability. Both machines use SINGER motors with similar speed and stitch outputs. The *Sewhandy* has a slightly higher maximum speed because of the pulley size. However, the FEATHERWEIGHT does have a reverse.

The hinged table on the FEATHERWEIGHT gives a larger platform for sewing than the *Sewhandy*. However, that same hinged table makes the FEATHERWEIGHT more fragile than the *Sewhandy*.

Stitch quality is similar. Foot pedal operation is similar. Tension adjustment and top threading is similar. Bobbin loading is similar, but bobbin case insertion is much more difficult with the *Sewhandy*. If your hands are large, it almost becomes impossible.

The FEATHERWEIGHT is slightly lighter, but is not as well balanced as the *Sewhandy*.

After everything is considered, the two machines are really too close to say that one is better than the other.... However, I would say that the FEATHERWEIGHT is a little more civilized than the *Sewhandy*.

Come to your own conclusion by sewing on both.... You might be surprised.

CARRYING CASE

Aug. 30, 1932.   F. OSANN ET AL   1,875,177

PORTABLE SEWING MACHINE CARRYING CASE

Filed May 21, 1929

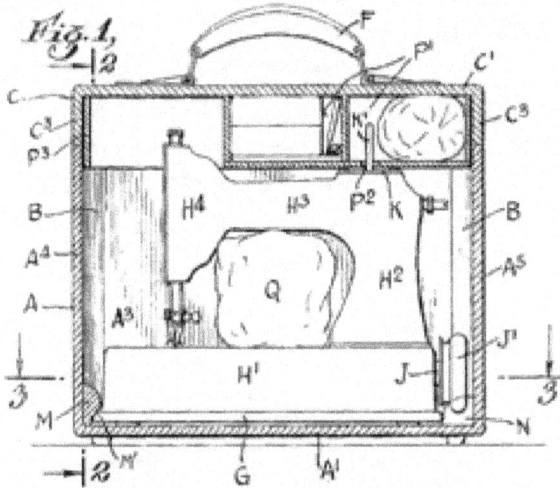

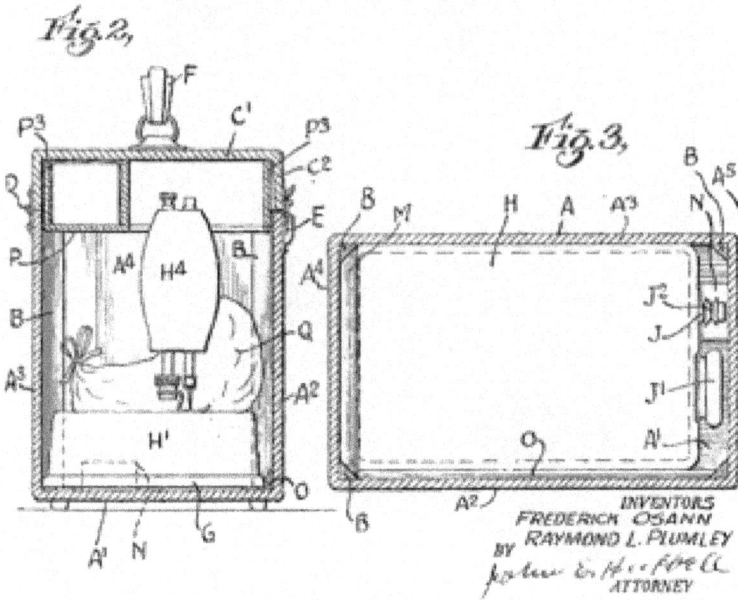

Fig. 1,

Fig. 2,

Fig. 3,

INVENTORS
FREDERICK OSANN
RAYMOND L. PLUMLEY
BY
ATTORNEY

151

The design for the Sewhandy Carrying Case is shown on the previous page. Note that the date of application for US Patent is May 21, 1929.

The Sewhandy Carrying Case is made of wood and covered in leatherette. The majority of the cases are a black color, but there are also a small number in tan. The case is about the same size as the SINGER Featherweight Type One, except that it is about ¾ inch shorter in height. The case dimensions are 13.25" wide x 8.125" deep x 10.875" high, and it weighs empty 4.5 pounds.

Carrying Case Exterior

The case has a removable wooden divided tray.

It has two brass hinges on the back, and two brass latches and a center brass key latch on the front. The earlier brass latches (STANDARD) were made by Eagle Lock Company, Terryville, Conn. It also has a black leather handle.

The later brass latches (OSSAN-SINGER and GENERAL ELECTRIC) were made by Langenau Manufacturing Company of Cleveland.

The earlier center latch (STANDARD) was made in Germany by SOSY Corporation of New York and marked Pat. Pending.

The later center latch (OSANN-SINGER and GENERAL ELECTRIC) was made in Germany by SOSY Corporation of New York and marked Pat 1717930.(Patented June 18, 1929)

Carrying Case Interior

The case inside is lined in a gold fabric throughout the case. On the later STANDARD Sewhandy, the top inner liner has a red fabric with the Standard winged logo.

With the OSANN-SINGER Sewhandy, the top inner liner is a gold fabric with the Sewhandy logo.

STANDARD
Sewhandy
THE STANDARD
SEWING MACHINE COMPANY
CLEVELAND, OHIO U.S.A.

The **GENERAL ELECTRIC** Model-A carrying case has an inner liner of gold fabric with the GE Merchandise Dept. label.

GE
GENERAL ELECTRIC
COMPANY
MERCHANDISE DEPT.
BRIDGEPORT, CONN.

All the carrying cases had an instructional label attached at the factory explaining how to correctly place the Sewhandy into the case. An example of this label is shown below.

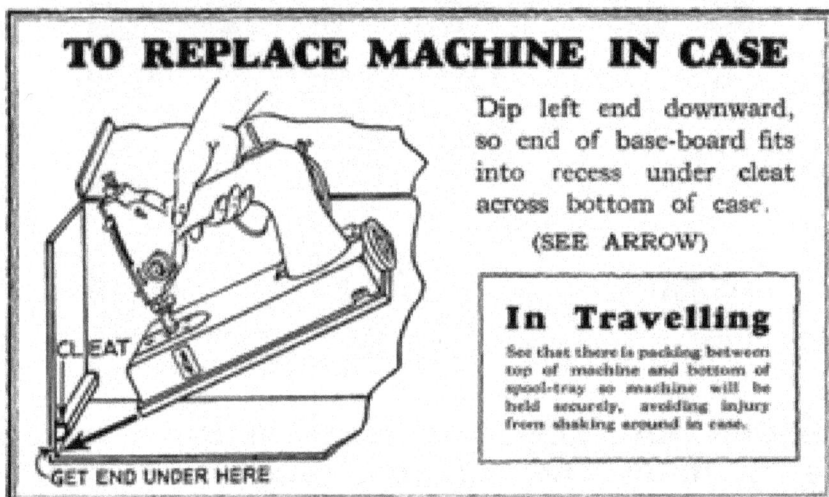

TO REPLACE MACHINE IN CASE

Dip left end downward, so end of base-board fits into recess under cleat across bottom of case.

(SEE ARROW)

In Travelling

See that there is packing between top of machine and bottom of spool-tray so machine will be held securely, avoiding injury from shaking around in case.

CLEAT

GET END UNDER HERE

Form 99

REMOVE THIS PASTER AFTER READING

EXTENSION TABLE

In 1936, the original designer of the Sewhandy, Richard K. Hohmann designed an extension table to fit on the Sewhandy bed. SINGER owned the Sewhandy production thru its dummy OSANN CORPORATION since 1934, and apparently was not interested. Or maybe they felt that it would make the Sewhandy more competitive with their Model 221 Featherweight.

No one really knows. For whatever reason, the Sewhandy extension table was never mass-produced or offered for sale to the public.

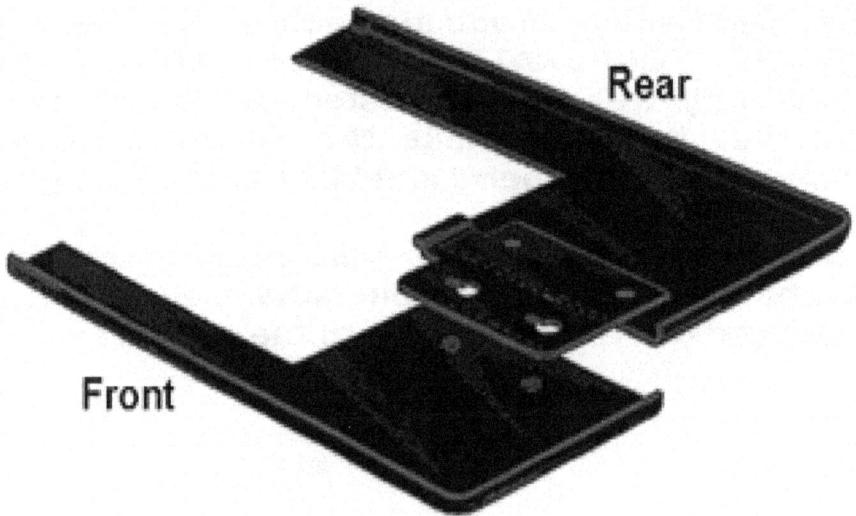

Rear

Front

The design was made up of two pieces that when assembled made up the u-shaped extension table. This two-piece design ensured that the extension table easily and safely fit in to the carrying case with the Sewhandy.

OPERATING INSTRUCTIONS

This chapter is for those of you that did not get the Operating Instructions with your *Sewhandy*.

Read These Valuable Suggestions Regarding Your New "*Sewhandy*" Sewing Machine

You now possess one of the most modern Electric Sewing Machines ever designed for home sewing.

In order that you may obtain the utmost enjoyment and service from your "SEWHANDY," these suggestions and instructions have been carefully prepared especially for your use.

This booklet tells, in plain, easily understood language, how to get best results from your "SEWHANDY." Study this booklet and you will find fascinating pleasure in learning all about the marvelous things your "SEWHANDY" will do, and how easy it is to use and enjoy. Should you require any further information, feel free to write us.

THE
Standard Sewing Machine Co.
CLEVELAND, OHIO
U. S. A.

1

How to Remove the Machine and Replace it in the Carrying Case

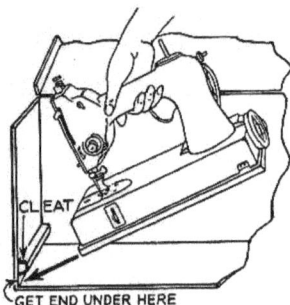

CLEAT

GET END UNDER HERE

FIRST remove the tray which contains the attachments, etc., tip the right end of the machine upward as shown in the above cut, and it will then lift out easily. To replace the machine in the case, tip the left end downward as shown, so that the end of the baseboard will fit into the recess under the cleat across the bottom of the case, as indicated by the arrow.

When packing the machine for traveling, be sure to place the piece of corrugated paper around the spool pin and between the spool plate and the underside of the tray, so that the machine will be held down securely by the latter when the lid of the case is closed.

Always keep the rheostat, when not in use, in the cloth bag prepared for it and place it on the bed of the machine under the arm, when putting the machine back into the case, to avoid scratching the enamel.

2

To Connect the Machine With Electric Current

TWO pieces of connection cord are packed with each machine. One of these cords has attached to it the foot control, or rheostat. Place the rheostat on the floor and plug the other end of the cord into the opening marked "Q" (Fig. 1), page 4. The other current supply cord has a flat plug on one end and a round plug on the other. Insert the flat plug into the opening in the bed of the machine marked "current connection," (Fig. 2), page 5. The other end of this wire has the round combination plug which can be screwed into any electric light socket or may be inserted into a floor or baseboard electric current outlet by pulling the screw part of the plug off, and inserting the two prongs of the plug into the outlet.

When you have finished sewing, always disconnect the supply cord from the house electric outlet and also from the machine.

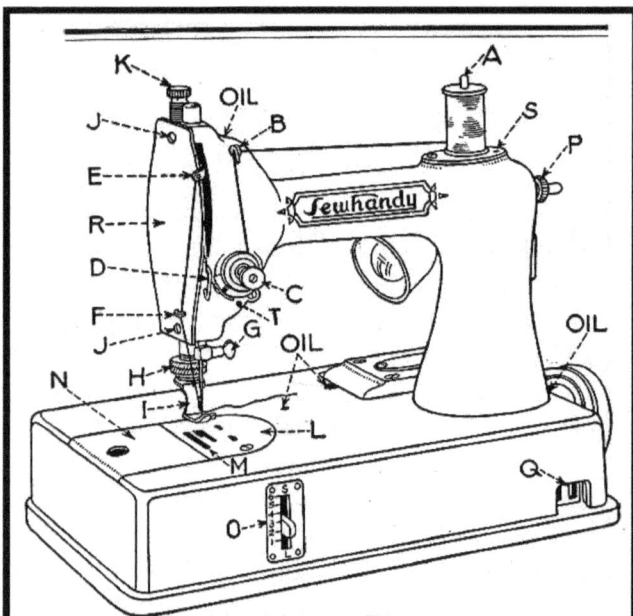

Front View—Figure 1

A   Spool Pin
B   Thread Guide
C   Tension
D   Thread Guide
E   Take-up
F   Thread Guide
G   Needle Clamp Screw
H   Presser Foot Nut
I   Presser Foot
J   Face Plate Screws
K   Presser Bar Cap Screw
L   Needle Plate
M   Feed
N   Slide Plate
O   Stitch Regulator
P   Bobbin Winder
Q   Foot Control Connection
R   Face Plate
S   Top Arm Cover
T   Spring Take-up

4

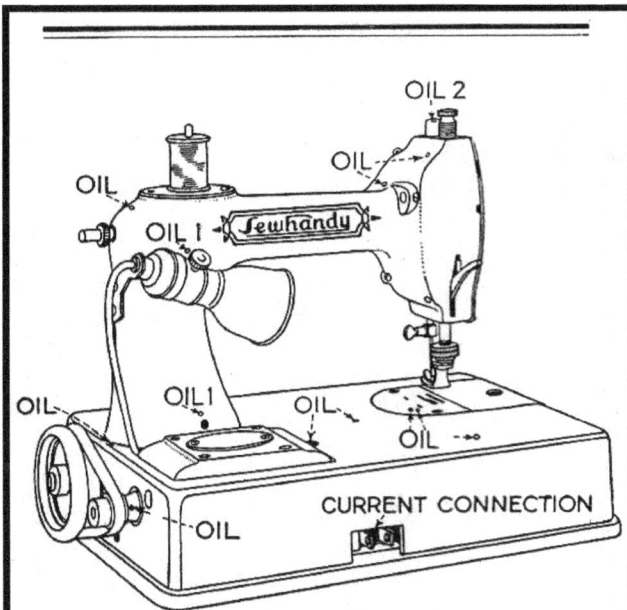

Rear View—Figure 2

Oiling Instructions

CAUTION! Use only the best light sewing machine oil, which can be purchased from the store or dealer where you obtained your "SEWHANDY" machine.

Oil moving parts frequently, as shown by oiling places indicated plainly on Fig. 2. All oiling places are easy to get at without removing the base of the machine.

In oiling through holes marked "Oil 1," Fig. 2, push the spout of the oil can all the way in against the shaft. *This is important.*

To oil the needle bar connection and the lower needle bar bearing, it will be necessary to remove the bottom screw "J" on the face plate "R" (Fig. 1) and loosen the

5

163

top screw, also "J," so that the face plate can be swung out of the way as shown in Fig. 3, to permit oiling these parts. The upper needle bar bearing is oiled through the hole marked "Oil 2," Fig. 2.

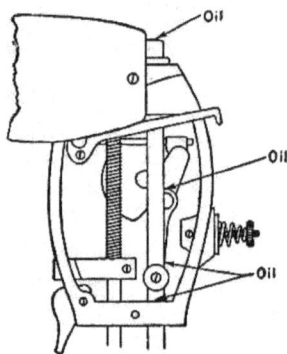

Figure 3

Use only a *few drops* of oil on each of these parts as, if too much oil is used, the surplus will be likely to drip on to and stain the fabric being stitched.

To oil the hook, take the bobbin case out and *put a drop or two of oil on the bobbin case bearing* surface of the hook. This should be done each time you start to use the machine, and if the machine is run steadily all day, should be done two or three times during that time. After this oiling, sew a minute or two on a piece of waste goods to absorb any surplus oil that may be on the hook.

Do not oil the gears. These are lubricated with a special grease at the factory and should not need attention for at least a year, and when they do, ordinary vaseline may be used.

Method of Threading the Spool Thread

THE correct method of threading is very simple, as shown by front view (Fig. 1). Place the spool on the spool pin "A," loop the thread into the guide "B," then down to the right of and between the tension discs "C," then into the loop of the spring take-up "T," then the guide "D" and up and through the take-up "E," then down through the thread guide "F" and thread through the eye of the needle from left to right.

To Remove the Bobbin Case

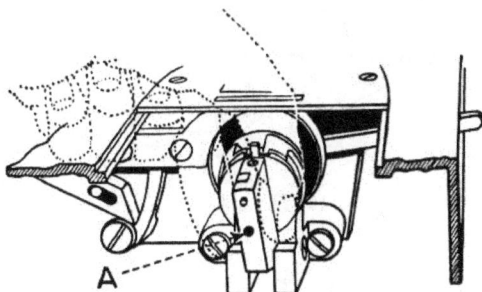

Figure 4

TURN the machine by hand until the take-up "E" (Fig. 1) is at its highest point. Raise the presser foot, remove any fabric you may have in the machine and cut the threads loose from the same. Pull the slide plate "N" (Fig. 1) to the left. This will provide sufficient opening in which to insert the thumb and forefinger of the left hand. Press the retaining latch "A" (Fig. 4) with the finger until the bobbin case retainer "B" (Fig. 5) falls back and then lift the bobbin case out, as shown in that figure.

7

165

To Remove the Bobbin from the Case

THROUGH the two large semi-circular openings "C" (Fig. 5) in the front of the bobbin case, press out the bobbin until you can grasp the rim with the thumb and finger and pull it out.

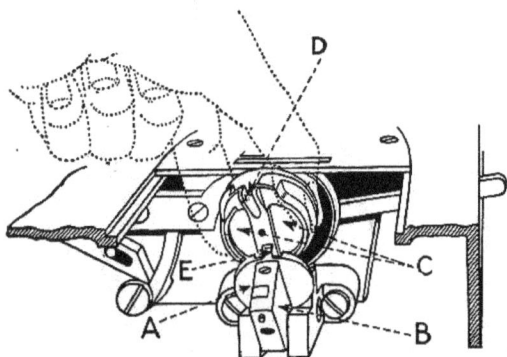

Figure 5

To Wind the Bobbin (See Fig. 6)

RAISE the presser foot "I" (Fig. 1) and see that the bobbin case is out of the machine, then place the bobbin on the winder "P" (Fig. 1) as shown in Fig. 6. Now draw some thread from the spool and wind the end around the bobbin three or four times by hand toward you, then hold the thread with the forefinger and keep a gentle pressure on it with the thumb, as shown in Fig. 6. Now start the machine with the foot as in sewing and run at a moderate speed until the bobbin is wound, not quite full. Never wind the bobbin full, as the thread is liable to slip off the rim and break in sewing.

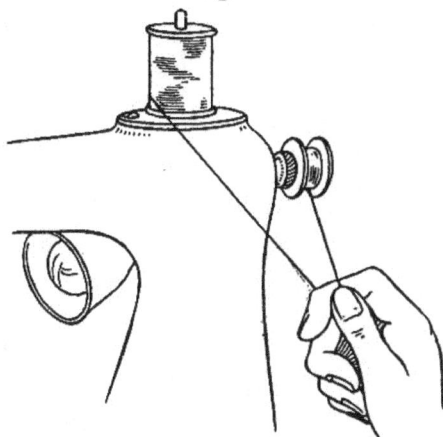

Figure 6

To Insert the Bobbin in the Case

PLACE the hole in the bobbin over the stem of the bobbin case and press it down into the case until the rim is below the edge of the case and the bobbin turns freely.

CAUTION! Always put the bobbin in the bobbin case so the thread will unwind in the direction of the arrow (Fig. 7).

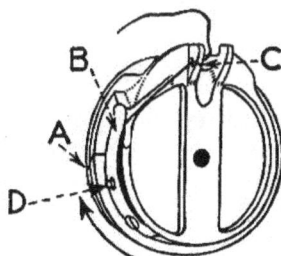

Figure 7

To Thread the Bobbin Case
(See Fig. 7)

WITH the bobbin inserted in the case so that the thread will unwind in the direction of the arrow as instructed, draw the thread through the slit "A," then under the tension spring "B" and thread through the hole "C." Now test the strength of the tension as per instructions for regulating the bobbin case tension. See page 11.

To Replace the Bobbin Case in the Machine

BE SURE to have the take-up and needle bar at their high position, then lay the bobbin case against the plate "A" (Fig. 5) with its forked part "D" (Fig. 5) over the holding tongue "E" of the plate "A," and close the latch "B" until it is firmly locked in place. If the latch will not lock securely you may be sure the bobbin case is not in its proper position.

CAUTION! The machine should never be started or run with the bobbin case in place until the latch is closed and securely locked.

Tensions

Perfect stitching depends largely upon the thread being drawn evenly into the fabric so it will look alike on both sides as shown in Fig. 8. To secure the proper tension do the following:

Figure 8

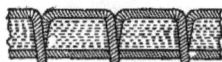

Figure 9

Figure 10

First—Regulate the Bobbin Tension.

Take hold of thread (Fig. 7) and pull out about six inches. Hold case suspended by thread. If case slips down, adjustment is too loose. Use small screw driver and adjust screw "D" (Fig. 7) slightly until the case will sustain itself when held still, but when jiggled a little, will gradually slide down the thread. This is the proper bobbin case tension adjustment, and it is rarely necessary to change it after it has been properly adjusted.

Second—Regulate Top Tension.

Turn the regulating nut "C" (Fig. 1) to the right to tighten and to the left to loosen this tension.

Sew on a piece of cloth and examine stitch. If the thread is straight along under side of fabric as in Fig. 9 then tighten the top tension "C" (Fig. 1) until stitch is the same on both sides of the fabric as shown in Fig. 8.

If the thread is straight along the top of fabric (Fig. 10), then loosen top tension slightly until stitch is the same on both sides of fabric as shown in Fig. 8.

11

To Regulate the Pressure Foot

TO regulate the pressure of the Presser Foot on the goods, adjust Presser Bar Cap Screw "K" (Fig. 1.) Turning this screw to the right will increase the pressure and to the left will lessen the pressure. The pressure should never be more than enough to feed the goods evenly. Light goods require less and heavy goods more pressure.

Stitch Regulation

THE length of the stitch is regulated by the stitch regulator "O" (Fig. 1). Move it up to shorten, and down to lengthen the stitch.

An Exclusive *"Sewhandy"* Feature

THE "SEWHANDY" Machine cannot clog. Its improved round bobbin and open hook mechanism preclude the possibility of this common cause of complaint. Any accumulation of thread or lint can be removed quickly and easily.

To Set the Needle

TO INSERT and adjust the needle; first, be sure the needle is *straight* and has a *sharp point*. Turn the machine by hand until the needle bar is at its highest point. Hold the needle in the left hand with the flat side toward the right and loosen the needle clamp screw "G" (Fig. 1). Insert needle as far as possible. Now, tighten the clamp screw "G" down solid on the needle and test its security by trying to pull the needle out of the bar, which you should not be able to do.

CAUTION! It is very important that the needle be pushed up as far as it will go into the bar and that it be securely held with the clamp screw against the danger of coming out and breaking and injuring the sewing mechanism, in operation.

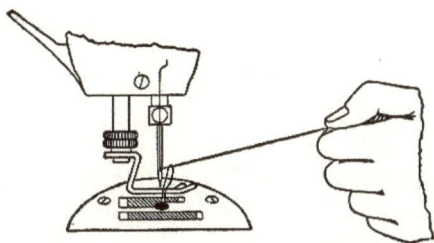

Fig. 11

To Prepare for Sewing

BEING sure that machine is threaded according to instructions, hold the end of the needle thread with the left hand, leaving it slack from the hand to the needle. Turn the hand wheel away from you until the needle moves down and up again to its highest point. Then pull the needle thread taut and the bobbin thread will be drawn up through the needle hole in the plate as shown in Fig. 11. Lay both threads back under the presser foot and close the slide plate "N" (Fig. 1). Place the fabric under the presser foot, lower the same and you are ready to sew.

Operation

START the machine by pressing the foot on the rheostat. Should the machine fail to start because of heavy material or thick seams, keep the foot on the rheostat and at the same time give the hand wheel a slight turn away from you.

Speed

THE speed of the machine is very easily controlled by the pressure of the foot on the rheostat. More pressure giving greater speed, less pressure giving less speed.

Needles and Threads

IN SELECTING the thread and needle for the fabric to be sewed, refer to the following Table:

Material	Thread	Needle
Crepe, Georgette and Light Silk	90–100 Cotton O Silk	#11
Muslin, Cotton Goods, Medium Weight Silk and Linen	60–80 Cotton A-B Silk	#14
Heavy Cotton, Linen, Light Woolen, Heavy Silk	40–60 Cotton C Silk	#16
Heavy Woolens, Clothing, Coats, etc.	30–40 Cotton D Silk	#18

Best results are obtained with the best soft finished cotton and a good grade of sewing silk.

CAUTION! Be sure the needle to be used is straight and has a sharp point.

BE SURE TO USE ONLY GENUINE

Sewhandy

NEEDLES

15

Helpful Suggestions

IF THE top thread breaks, examine the needle to make sure it is not bent and that it has a perfectly sharp point; also be sure it is set up as far as it will go into the needle bar and securely tightened with the needle clamp screw "G" (Fig. 1). Or the machine may not be properly threaded: See threading instructions page 7. Or your tension may be too tight or the thread too large for the size of the needle: See table for needle and thread sizes on page 15.

If the machine skips stiches it is most likely caused by a bent or imperfect point needle or because the needle is not set fully up in the needle bar.

Needle breakage is usually caused by the presser foot or attachment not being securely fastened with the presser foot nut "H" (Fig. 1), or because point of the needle is damaged or by pulling the work while sewing.

If the machine runs heavy use a few drops of kerosene in the various oil holes and after running it a few minutes oil with good light sewing machine oil.

Attachments

The attachments are the best obtainable and if used carefully and according to directions, satisfactory work will result.

Directions for Use of Attachments

HEMMING

RAISE the presser foot and needle bar; attach the hemmer in place of the presser foot (see cut). Insert the edge of the cloth in the hemmer, folded as shown; draw the cloth far enough through the hemmer so the needle will enter its extreme edge. Let the hemmer foot down and proceed to sew, guiding the work and keeping the scroll of the hemmer just full.

Any width of hem can be made with the hemmer and feller, by folding the goods the desired width of hem and passing the edge through as in narrow hemming.

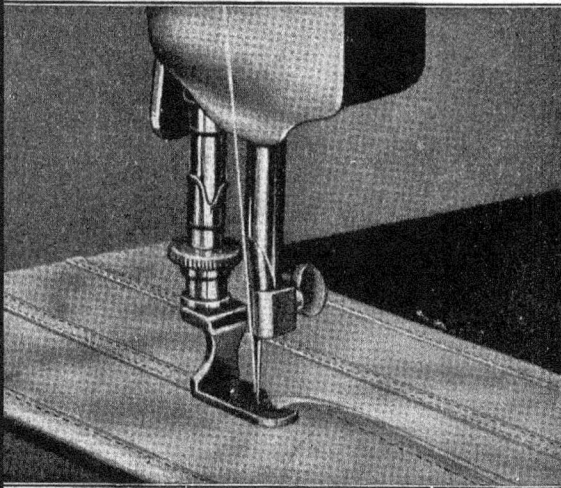

Hemming and Felling

17

Hemming and Felling

The hemmer is also the feller. Stitch two pieces together, their edges to the right, and the lower edge projecting about 1/4 inch beyond the upper, then open the work out flat edges up; draw the edges at the beginning of the seam into the hemmer, and proceed to sew, as in cut on page 17. French seams suitable for curve or body seams can also be made with the feller by inserting two pieces with edges even.

Hemming and Sewing on Lace

The hemmer and feller which accompanies this machine is made with a slot for the needle to pass through instead of a round hole. This slot is to enable the operator to make a hem and sew on lace at the same time. Start a narrow hem and pass the end of the lace through the slot in the side of the hemmer, carrying it under the back

Hemming and Sewing On Lace, One Operation

18

of the hemmer and on top of the hem, as in cut on page 18; then proceed as in ordinary hemming. Keep the lace well in the slot so that the needle will catch it every time.

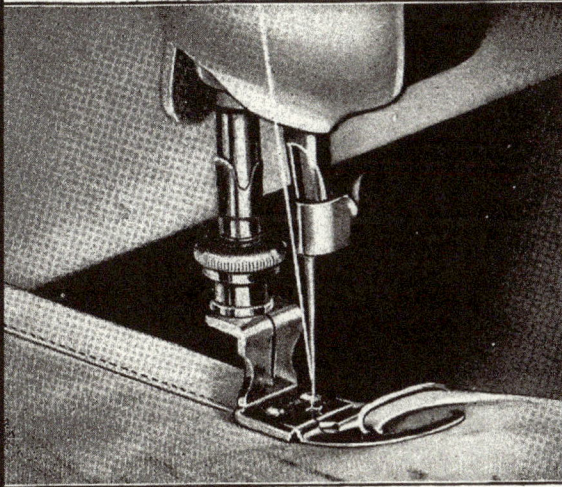

Wide Hemming

Wide Hemming

THE wide hemmers belong to the regular set of attachments, and are used for wide hemming and on heavy goods. Attach in place of presser foot. Fold the goods (by hand) the width of hem required, turning one fold only, adding about one-eighth of an inch, which will be turned under by the hemmer; introduce the edge of the cloth the same as for a narrow hem, and proceed in the same way, holding the goods in the right hand.

19

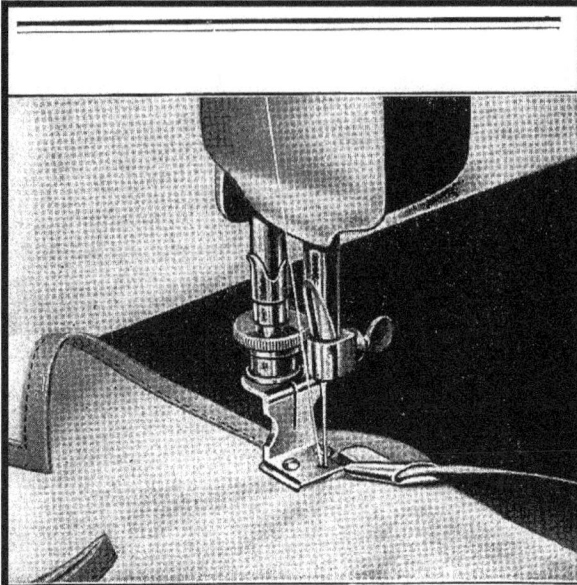

Binding

Binding

RAISE the presser bar and the needle. Attach the binder in place of the presser foot.

Pass the binding through the scroll of the binder and draw it back under the needle. Place the edge of the goods to be bound between the scrolls of the binder and draw it under the needle. Lower the presser bar and sew as usual.

For bias binding, goods of any description can be used. For the binder ordinarily used, the binding should be cut seven-eighths of an inch wide, in order to turn under at the edges.

20

To Bind With Common Dress Braid

PROCEED the same as when using bias binding, as explained above. The only difference is, the dress braid being narrower, the edges will not be turned under, as is the case with bias binding.

To Bind Scallops

IN BINDING scallops, after binding around the scallops, stop the machine with the needle in the goods, fold the elbow or angle of the following scallop so as to form as nearly as possible a straight line, and continue binding. Hold the goods being bound, a little firmer than the binding, which will prevent its being drawn.

To Make French Folds

ATTACH the binder as usual. Pass the binding through the binder and sew as usual, stitching the edges together. This can be sewed on at the same time if desired.

TUCKING

To Attach Tucker to Machine

ATTACH the tucker firmly to the presser bar in place of the foot; see that the lever which works the creasing arm is under the needle clamp screw.

21

To Adjust the Tucker

LOOSEN the thumb-screw. The *width of the tuck* is regulated by the distance of the edge-guide to the right of the line of the needle or seam; the tuck will be exactly as wide as this distance. *The space between tucks* is determined by the distance of the

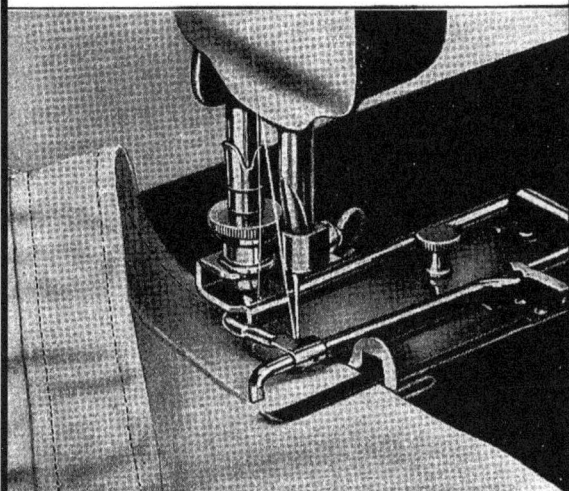

Tucking

creasing blade to the left of the line of the needle or seam.

The figures on the scales on the tucker are for convenience in adjusting the width of tuck and distance between tucks. If the guides on the two scales are at the same figure (to the right), then the creasing blade is twice the distance to the left of the needle that the edge-guide is to the right, and the tucks will meet; that is, the crease of one tuck will lie exactly over the seam of the last tuck. When adjusted as wanted, tighten thumb-screw.

To Operate Tucker

MAKE the first crease in the usual manner by hand. Insert the cloth between the creasing arm and blade and the blade spring; the part that is to be tucked on the top. Draw it to the right until the crease of the cloth comes against the edge-guide. Then sew as in plain work. Fold at the crease in making subsequent tucks. Take care that the tuck last made is inside the gauge that is directly beneath the creaser blade.

RUFFLING

To Attach the Ruffler

RAISE the presser bar and needle, remove the presser foot and put the ruffler in its place, adjust so that the needle passes through the center of the hole in the foot, and the prongs of the fork will be on either side of the needle clamp. Fasten firmly in place. Use an occasional drop of oil on the fork lever hinge.

Plain Ruffling

To Operate Ruffler

INSERT the goods to be ruffled between the blued blades, pushing the cloth from you with the aid of the small screwdriver or stiletto, until it lies smoothly under the needle, over first but under second guide. Drop the presser bar and proceed as in plain sewing. To make a very full ruffle, shorten the stitch and turn the thumb-screw or disc to the left until you have the desired amount of fullness. To make wide plaits, turn thumb-screw to the left until it stops, then lengthen the stitch to match; the length of stitch should be regulated so that the plaits will lie evenly and not pile upon each other, or lie too far apart. To make fine scant gathers, use short stitch and regulate ruffller by turning thumb-screw or disc to the right until the blued blade moves back enough to just catch the goods, thus making the finest possible ruffle.

Ruffling and Sewing On

PLACE goods below both blued blades on feed of machine and up over first guide. Place material to be ruffled as in "plain ruffling," under second guide. Proceed as in plain sewing, being careful to keep the goods smooth and straight.

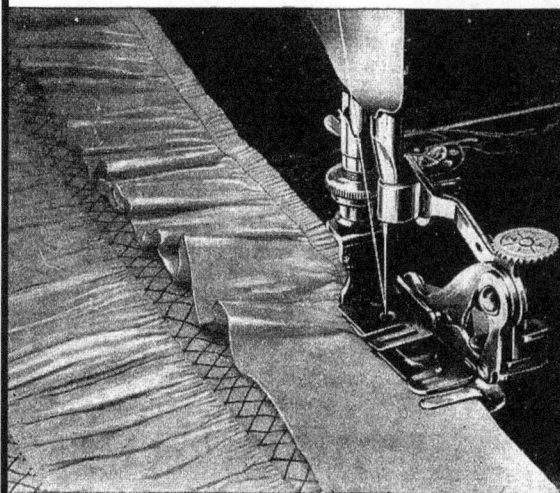

Ruffling and Sewing On

Sewing On Ruffle With Narrow Heading

FOLD over edge to be gathered ½ inch. Place material to be ruffled between blued blades, under second guide and over first guide. Place garment underneath the ruffler, allowing it to come to the left of the needle the width of the ruffle; this will make bottom of ruffle and bottom of garment perfectly even. Be sure to keep garment straight.

Ruffling, Sewing On and Putting On Facing at One Stitching Operation

PLACE goods and material to be ruffled exactly as in "ruffling and sewing on." Place facing over the blued blades and under the foot, and proceed as usual, being careful to keep goods and facing straight and smooth.

Underbraiding

Underbraider

USE the short prong braider foot in place of the regular presser foot. The underbraider is placed in position as follows: At the right of the presser foot you will see two openings. Place the point A in the opening farthest from you, and the pin C in the opening nearest

26

you. Push the attachment into these openings as far as it will go, which will fasten it. Before pushing it into place be careful to put the braid into the channel of the attachment with enough projecting from the end to insure its coming under the needle and presser foot. Place the goods wrong side up with the pattern traced on the upper side, and proceed as in ordinary sewing, following the pattern.

Underbraiding

185

Sewhandy

Portable Electric Family Sewing Machine
PARTS LIST

Part No.	Name
9000	Arm
9001	Arm Screw (3 used)
9026	Arm Dowels (2 used)
9003-A	Arm Cover Plate (Assem.)
9006	Arm Cover Plate Screw
9015	Arm Shaft (Top)
9024	Arm Shaft Miter Gear
9017	Arm Shaft Gear Set Screw (2 used)
9018	Arm Shaft Collar
9019	Arm Shaft Collar Set Screw
9020	Arm Shaft (Vertical)
9021	Arm Shaft Vertical Bushing (Upper)
9022	Arm Shaft Vertical Bushing (Lower)
9028	Arm Shaft Vertical Bushing Set Screw (2 used)
9024	Arm Shaft Vertical Miter Gear (Upper)
9017	Arm Shaft Vertical Miter Gear Screw (2 used)
9025	Arm Shaft Vertical Bevel Gear (Lower)
9026	Arm Shaft Vertical Bevel Gear Pin
9027-A	Arm Shaft Vertical Assembled with Gear and Pin
9040	Bed
9041	Bed Base
9042	Bed Base Screw (5 used)
9043	Bed Pads (Rubber) (4 used)
9044	Belt Wheel
9019	Belt Wheel Set Screw (2 used)
9045	Bobbin
9046	Bobbin Winder
9047	Bobbin Case
9048	Bobbin Case Tension Spring
9049	Bobbin Case Tension Spring Screw (Holding)
9050	Bobbin Case Tension Spring Screw (Adjusting)
9051	Bobbin Case Bobbin Retaining Spring
102-C	Bobbin Case Bobbin Retaining Spring Screw

PARTS LIST

Part No.	Name
9053-A	Bobbin Case, (Assem.)
9069-B	Bobbin Case Retainer
9055-B	Bobbin Case Retainer Bracket
9056	Bobbin Case Retainer Bracket Screw (2 used)
9075-AB	Bobbin Case Retainer Plate (Assem.)
9076	Bobbin Case Retainer Plate Stud Set Screw
9061	Bobbin Case Retainer Fulcrum Pin
9062	Bobbin Case Retainer Fulcrum Pin Set Screw
9063	Bobbin Case Retainer Fulcrum Pin Spring
9074	Bobbin Case Retainer Latch
9068-B	Bobbin Case Retainer Adjusting Screw
9073	Bobbin Case Retainer Latch Pin
9066	Bobbin Case Retainer Latch Spring
9067-AB	Bobbin Case Retainer, (Assem.)
9070	Belt (Rubber)
9080-A	Face Plate (Assem.)
9081-B	Face Plate Thread Guide
104-C	Face Plate Thread Guide Rivet
9006	Face Plate Screw (2 used)
9083	Feed Shaft
9087	Feed and Feed Lift Eccentric
9088	Feed Eccentric Screw
9089	Feed Eccentric Lever
9090	Feed Eccentric Lever Fulcrum Screw
9103-B	Feed Bar
9092	Feed Bar Spring
9093	Feed Bar Fulcrum Stud
9028	Feed Bar Fulcrum Stud Set Screw
9094-B	Feed Bar Operating Lever
9095-B	Feed Bar Operating Lever Fulcrum Screw
9096-B	Feed Point
9101-B	Feed Point Screw (2 used)
9098	Feed Shaft Gear
9017	Feed Shaft Gear Set Screw (2 used)
C-400	Gauge
9205	Gauge Screw

PARTS LIST

No. Part	Name
9110	Hook
4836	Hook Set Screw
9112-A	Hook Cover (Assem.)
9115	Hook Shaft
9116	Hook Shaft Bushing (Front)
9117	Hook Shaft Bushing (Rear)
9086	Hook Shaft Bushing Set Screw (2 used)
9118	Hook Shaft Spur Gear
9017	Hook Shaft Spur Gear Screw (2 used)
9119	Hook Shaft Bevel Gear
9017	Hook Shaft Bevel Gear Screw (2 used)
9125-A	Lamp Shade and Socket (Assem.)
9126	Lamp Shade Bracket
9127	Lamp Shade Bracket Screw
9128	Lamp Shade Socket Clamp Screw
9129-B	Motor Screws (2 used)
B9129-B	Motor Screw Washer (2 used)
9432	Motor Cover Plate
9433	Motor Cover Plate Screw (4 used)
9434	Motor Pulley
9435	Motor Pulley Set Screw
9130-B	Needle Bar
9131	Needle Bar Cap
9133	Needle Bar Crank
9134	Needle Bar Crank Set Screw
9135	Needle Bar and Take-up Crank
9136	Needle Bar and Take-up Crank Pin
9137-A	Needle Bar Crank and Take-up Crank, (Assem.)
9138	Needle Bar Link
9139	Needle Bar Yoke
9019	Needle Bar Yoke Screw
9140-B	Needle Clamp
311-C	Needle Clamp Screw
9141	Needle Plate
9142	Needle Plate Screw (2 used)
9179	Oil Tube

PARTS LIST

Part No.	*Name*
9150	Presser Bar
9151	Presser Bar Spring
B316D	Presser Bar Spring Adjusting Cap
9152	Presser Bar Guide
9153	Presser Bar Guide Screw
9154	Presser Bar Lifter
9155	Presser Bar Lifter Screw
323-C	Presser Foot
325	Presser Foot Nut
324-F	Presser Foot Thumb Nut
9165-A	Stitch Regulating Lever (Assem.)
9166	Stitch Regulating Lever Fulcrum Screw
9168	Stitch Indicating Plate
9169	Stitch Indicating Plate Rivet (4 used)
9180	Take-up Crank
9181	Take-up Lever
9182	Take-up Lever Screw
9183	Take-up Yoke Rod
9184	Take-up Yoke Rod Set Screw
9185-A	Take-up, (Assem.)
9186	Take-up Yoke
9187	Take-up Fulcrum Stud
9019	Take-up Fulcrum Stud Set Screw
9188	Tension Stud
9189	Tension Stud Set Screw
9190	Tension Nut
9191	Tension Spring
F.O.129	Tension Disc (2 used)
9193	Tension Release Plate
9194	Tension Release Pin
9195	Tension Release Lever
9196	Tension Release Lever Fulcrum Stud
9028	Tension Release Lever Fulcrum Stud Set Screw
9198	Tension Spring Take-up
9201	Thread Cutter
9199	Thread Guide (Upper)
9200	Thread Guide (Lower)

SUMMARY

This brings to a close this book "before the Featherweight – Sewhandy Volume 1 History".

I hope that you found reading it both enjoyable and educational.

For more detailed information about preventative maintenance and repair of the *Sewhandy*, be sure to read my book "before the Featherweight – Sewhandy Volume 2 Maintenance & Repair". You will find a short preview of Volume 2 beginning on page 193 of this book.

Reference and Bibliography information available on request.

If you have any questions about this book or the Sewhandy sewing machine, visit my website:

www.SewhandySewingMachine.com

You can also email me at <u>Dar-Bet@att.net</u> .

For information about other books I have written, visit my website:

www.DarrelKaiserBooks.com

PERSONAL MACHINE DIARY

DATE	MODEL	SN	PURCHASE INFORMATION

PREVIEW

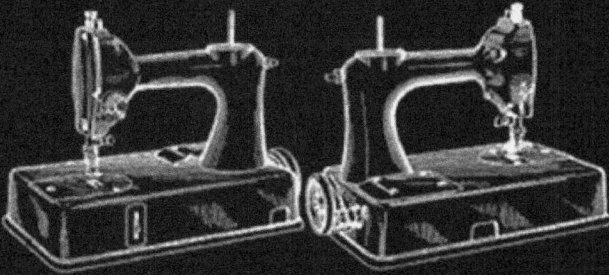

before the
Featherweight

Sewhandy
Volume 2
Maintenance
& Repair

Darrel P. Kaiser

ISBN 978-0-6151-6967-5

Chapter Titles

- **THE FIRST** *Sewhandy*

- **IDENTIFYING YOUR** *Sewhandy*

- **STANDARD** *Sewhandy*

- **FREDERICK OSANN COMPANY** *Sewhandy*

- **GENERAL ELECTRIC** *MODEL A*

- **OSANN Corp SINGER** *Sewhandy*

- **MODEL SPECIFICATIONS**

- *Sewhandy* **MANUAL**

- **MECHANICAL OPERATION**

- **ELECTRICAL OPERATION**

- **PREVENTATIVE MAINTENANCE**
- **LUBRICATION**

- **MOTOR DISASSEMBLY & BRUSH REPLACEMENT**

- **TROUBLESHOOTING & REPAIR**

- *Sewhandy* **TROUBLESHOOTING**

- **TENSION & YOUR** *Sewhandy*

- **TIMING YOUR** *Sewhandy*

- **REPLACING CONSUMABLES**

- *Sewhandy* **PARTS**

- **MAJOR REPAIRS**

- **SALVAGING A** *Sewhandy*

- **RESTORE or not RESTORE**

- **BUYING A** *Sewhandy*

- **SHIPPING YOUR** *Sewhandy*

- **COMPARISON SPECIFICATIONS**

PREFACE

Volume 2 provides preventative maintenance and repair information for all the *Sewhandy* models (including GE Model A) using modern lubricants, components, and techniques. Also included are detailed Mechanical and Electrical Operation, and Troubleshooting Chapters.

MECHANICAL OPERATION

Note: This is a short preview of the Volume 2 Chapter on Mechanical Operation. This chapter in Volume 2 is actually 14 pages long.

The *Sewhandy* mechanical operation follows the normal sewing machine mechanical arrangement used in the 1920's.

It has a low rear motor providing power thru a rubber belt to the Belt Wheel. The Belt Wheel is mechanically connected to the Hook Shaft. Note that the Belt or Hand Wheel is mounted low on the *Sewhandy*. Compare this to the SINGER Featherweight Model 221 where it is high on the machine.

Theoretically, having the rotating mass of the Belt Wheel low on the machine creates a low center-of-gravity. This produces a more stable machine with less motor torque/speed change reaction and vibration.

In contrast, the newer (1933) design of the SINGER Featherweight Model 221 has the spinning mass of the Hand Wheel about 3.5 inches higher than the *Sewhandy*. Because of this the SINGER 221 has a much higher center-of-gravity and a lower stability factor.

The *Sewhandy* mechanical operation is broken down into three separate functional areas: 1) Shafts and Gears, 2) Needle Drive, and 3) Feed and Hook Drive.

Shafts and Gears

In operation, the motor and Belt Wheel rotate in a clockwise direction as viewed from the right side or front. Since the main drive shaft (Hook Shaft) is connected to the Belt Wheel, it also rotates in the clockwise direction. See the drawing below.

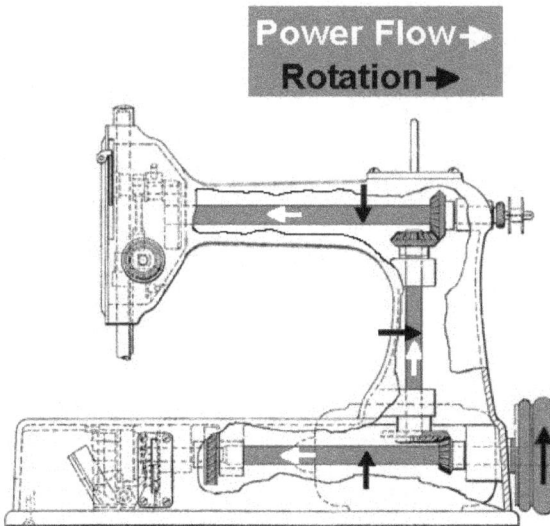

The 3/8th inch diameter Hook Shaft connects to the 5/16th inch diameter Arm Shaft (Vertical) thru a brass bevel gear set. The Arm Shaft (Vertical) rotates in a counter clockwise direction. It connects thru a brass miter gear set to the 5/16th inch diameter Arm Shaft (Top) that also rotates in counter clockwise direction (as viewed from the Belt Wheel end).

There are bushings and bushing supports for each drive shaft. Each bushing has its own oil hole to provide for lubrication replenishment. Oil hole location is identified in the Preventative Maintenance chapter. Bushing locations are shown in the drawing below.

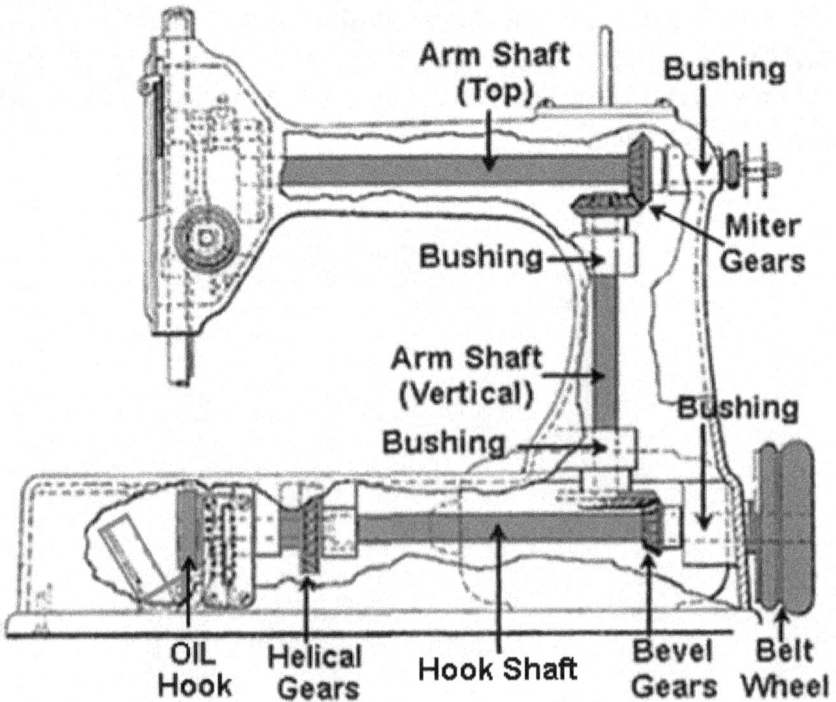

Arm Shaft (Top)　Bushing

Bushing　Miter Gears

Arm Shaft (Vertical)

Bushing

Bushing

OIL Hook　Helical Gears　Hook Shaft　Bevel Gears　Belt Wheel

The bevel gears on the Hook Shaft and Arm Shaft (Vertical) are straight cut gears with a gear ratio of 1:2 (18 teeth and 36 teeth). The Arm Shaft (Top) and Arm Shaft (Vertical) Miter Gears are a special type of straight cut bevel gear designed to operate in pairs with identical numbers of teeth (24) and diametrical pitch, and a 1:1 gear ratio. Brass gears are used because the constant meshing work hardens the teeth allowing them to last longer.

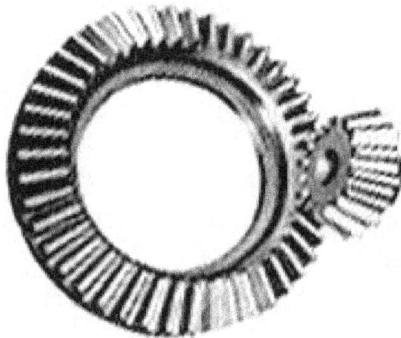

Bevel Gears

Miter Gears

Needle Drive

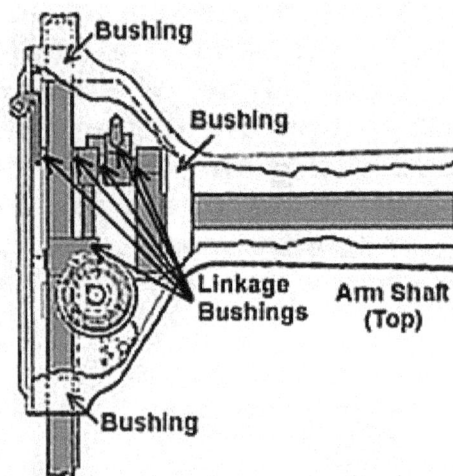

The counter clockwise rotating Arm Shaft (Top) provides power thru the bushing support to the Needle Bar and Take-up Crank. This connects and provides power to both the Needle Drive and the Take-up Lever.

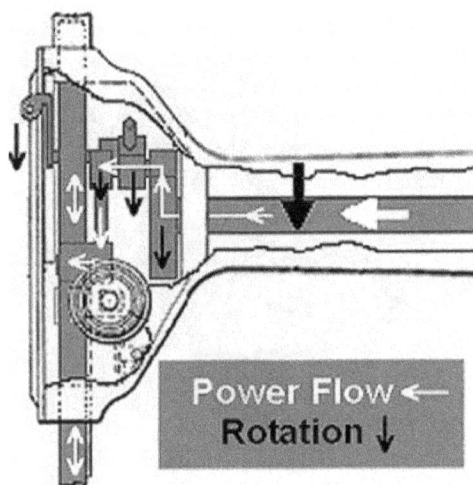

200

The Needle Drive power flow is shown below. The power flow is from the Needle Bar and Take-up Crank (larger right white arrow) thru the Take-up Yoke (larger left white arrow) thru the Needle Bar Yoke (thinner white arrow) thru the Needle Bar link thru the Needle Bar Clamp thru the Needle Bar (double headed white arrow) to the Needle. This process changes the Arm Shaft (Top) rotational movement into the up-down movement of the needle. It also maintains the exact timing relative to the Feed Shaft and Hook Drive.

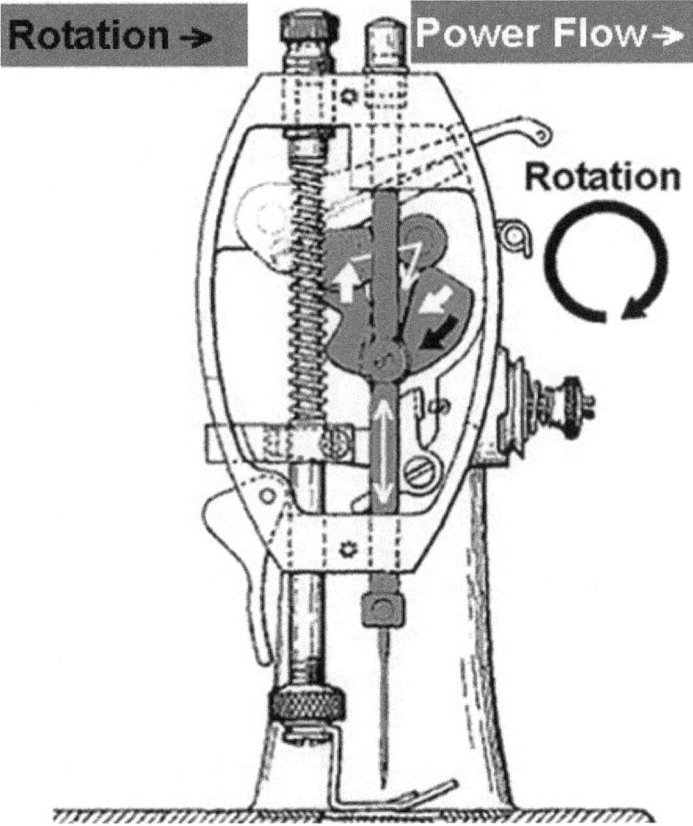

The Take-up Lever power flow is shown below. The power flow is from the Needle Bar and Take-up Crank (right white arrow) thru the Take-up Yoke (center white arrow) thru the Take-up Yoke Rod thru the Take-up Crank (left white arrow) thru the Take-up Fulcrum to the Take-up Lever. This process changes the Arm Shaft (Top) rotational movement into the up-down movement of the Take-up Lever. It also maintains the exact timing relative to the Feed Shaft and Hook Drive.

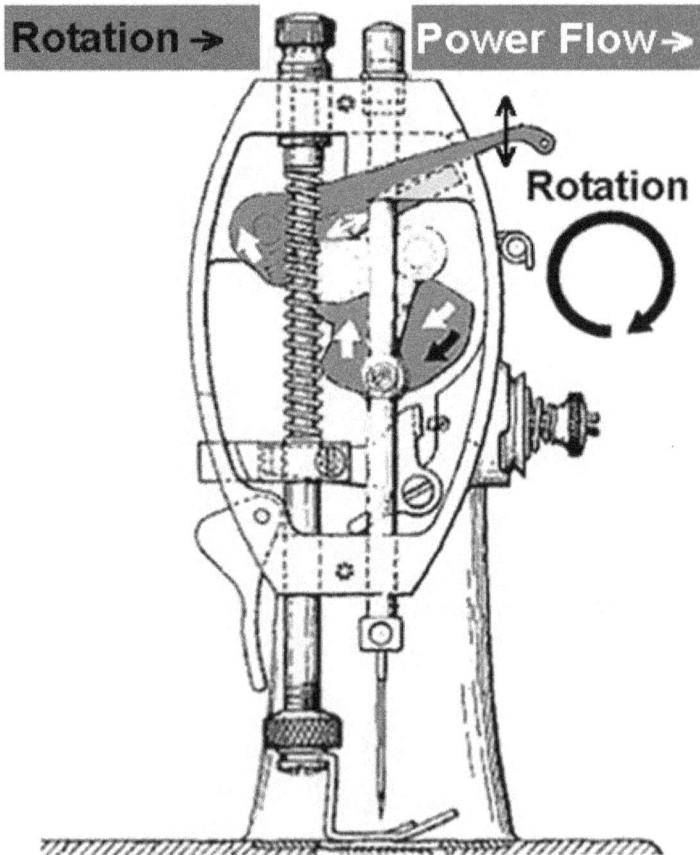

Rotation →   Power Flow →

Rotation

ELECTRICAL
OPERATION

Note: This is a short preview of the Volume 2
Chapter on Electrical Operation. This chapter in
Volume 2 is actually 17 pages long.

The *Sewhandy* has a fairly simple electrical
circuit. Note that the system, as manufactured,
does not use a polarized or grounded 3-prong
plug. There is always a risk of shock when using
these older electrical systems. (The *Sewhandy*
can be rewired to use the 3-prong grounded
system. Contact author by email for price). The
electrical system consists of the following:

- **Black Cloth covered two-conductor Main
  Power cord from the 120VAC wall outlet
  (male 2-prong plug) to the power input
  connector (female 2-prong plug).**
- **Rear input power connector (male 2 prong
  plug).**
- **Foot Pedal with two-conductor power cord
  connecting with front of machine (male 2-
  prong plug).**
- **Front Foot Pedal power connector (female
  2-prong plug).**
- **Black Cloth covered single conductor wire
  from Rear input power connector to Drive
  Motor.**
- **Black Cloth covered single conductor wire
  from Rear input power connector to Front
  Foot Pedal power connector (female 2-
  prong plug).**

- Black cloth covered two-conductor cord from Rear input power connector Lamp assembly.
- Black Cloth covered single conductor wire from Front Foot Pedal power connector (female 2-prong plug) to Drive Motor.
- Lamp Assembly with side rotary switch.
- Sewing Machine Drive Motor

Theory of Operation

Plug the Foot Pedal power cord 2–prong male connector into the front 2-prong female connector. Plug the machine female 2-prong connector on the Main Power cord into the male 2-prong connector on the rear of the machine. Plug the Main Power cord 2-prong male connector into a 120VAC power source, i.e. switched power strip. The *Sewhandy* is now ready to operate. It does not have a main power on-off switch.

You can test for power to the *Sewhandy* by turning the Lamp Assembly switch on. The light will now be lit. Pressing on the Foot Pedal will cause the Drive Motor to rotate.

How does all this work? The 120VAC *HOT* side current at the power strip moves thru the Main Power Cord to the Rear Input power connector. Here it connects with the *Hot* (Black) wire going to the Front Foot Pedal power connector. It also connects thru a two-conductor cord to the Lamp Assembly rotary switch. The *Hot* continues thru the Front Foot Pedal power cord to the Foot Pedal. The Foot Pedal has a Resistive Element that limits the current and the motor speed. The now variable current leaves the Foot Pedal out thru the Foot Pedal Power cord to the other contact of the 2-prong Front Foot Pedal power connector. The variable current continues thru the wire to the Drive Motor. The variable current is felt across the brushes and windings and causes the Drive Motor to spin if there is an electrical return or neutral path.

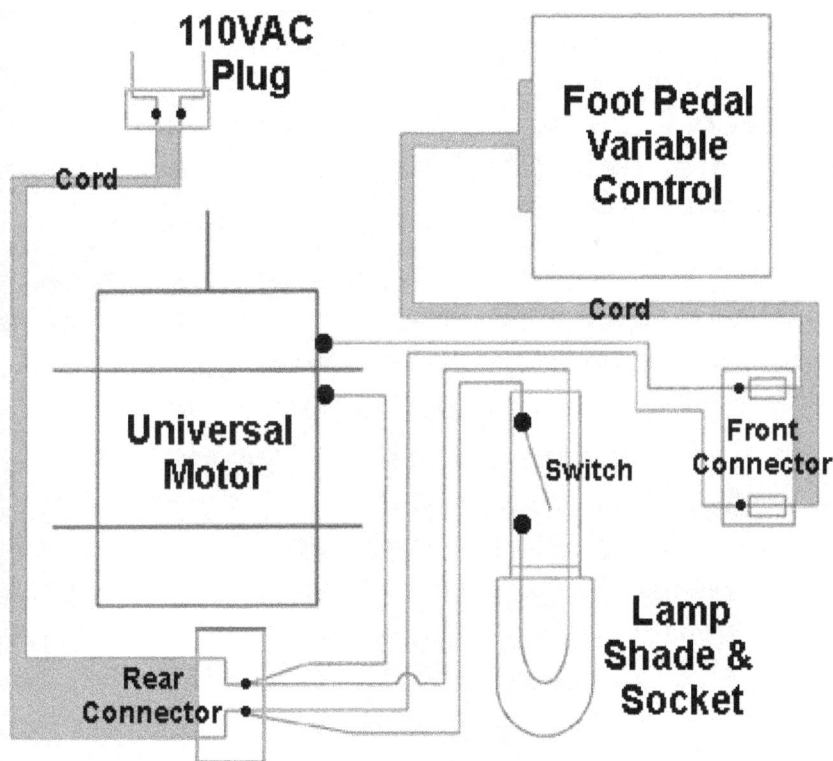

110VAC Plug

Foot Pedal Variable Control

Cord

Cord

Universal Motor

Switch

Front Connector

Rear Connector

Lamp Shade & Socket

The neutral path continues out of the Drive Motor thru the wire to the Rear Input power connector. The return path continues thru the Main Power cord to the 120VAC power strip neutral.

The Lamp Assembly circuit is powered from the *Hot* side of the Rear Input power connector as explained previously. The return or neutral for the Lamp Assembly is thru the other conductor of the two-conductor cord to the neutral side of the Rear Input power connector. As before, the return path continues thru the Main Power cord to the 120VAC power strip neutral.

Motor Theory & Breakdown

There are two different motors used on the *Sewhandy* and GE *MODEL A*. The GE motor is used on all models except for the OSANN SINGER *Sewhandy*. The OSANN SINGER *Sewhandy* uses a SINGER BRK/BUK series motor. Both motors are Universal type motors.

Universal Motors

GE and SINGER used the Universal or Commutator motor in the *Sewhandy* because the universal motor operates at much higher speeds than an induction motor and delivers more power than a similar size induction motor.

The universal motor is a single-phase commutated motor with wound field coils in series with a DC type armature (wound rotor). Universal motors can be powered by either DC or AC. The have a rotor or armature with coils of wire wound around it. They also have a rotating cylinder or commutator with alternating strips of conducting and nonconducting material.

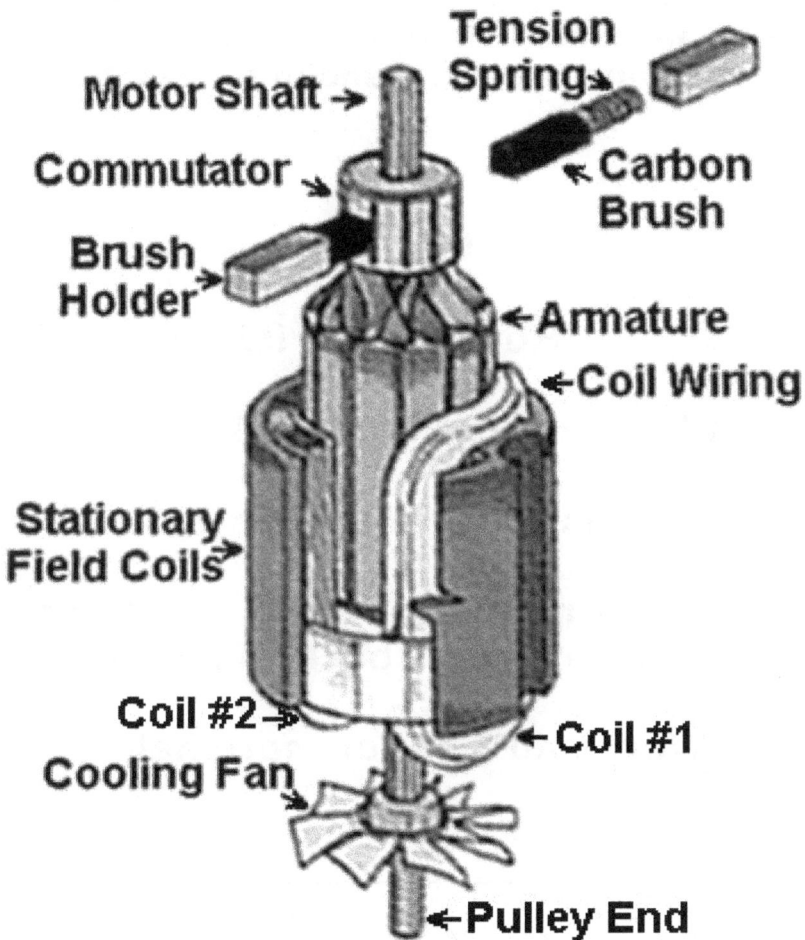

Tension Spring→

Motor Shaft →

Commutator ↘

↖Carbon Brush

Brush Holder→

←Armature

←Coil Wiring

Stationary Field Coils→

Coil #2→

←Coil #1

Cooling Fan↘

←Pulley End

The armature and the commutator are mounted on the motor shaft. A carbon brush on each side of the commutator transfers current from the electrical circuit. These brushes are soft blocks of carbon with a spring attached to provide slight pressure and compensate for wear. When the carbon brushes slip over the commutator surface, the armature is magnetized and rotates. This provides the rotation that powers the sewing machine. Most universal motors also have a cooling fan at the end of the shaft.

How does it work?

How do I fix it?

What lubrication does it need?

What does this wire do?

How does my motor come apart? And how do I get it back together?

Where do I go for more help?

Find out the answers to these questions and many more in the over 200 pages in Volume 2. Visit my websites:

www.SewhandySewingMachine.com

www.DarrelKaiserBooks.com

Books by Darrel P. Kaiser
www.DarrelKaiserBooks.com

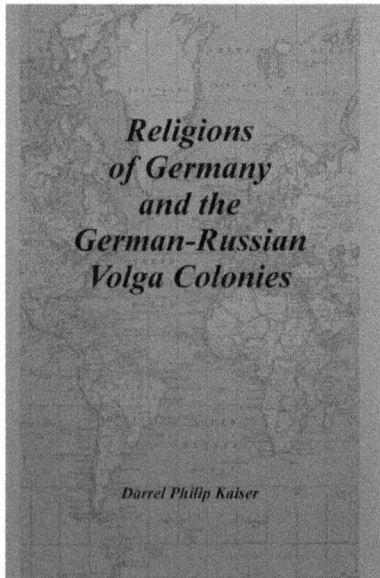

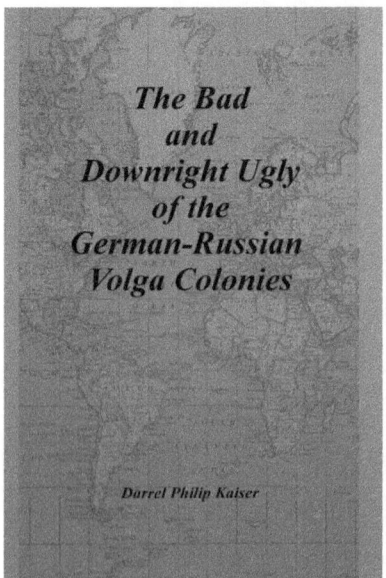

Origin & Ancestors
Families
Karle & Kaiser
of the
German-Russian Volga Colonies

Adolf	Heydmann	Raab
Andreas	Hieronymus	Rudolph
Arp	Horn	Schaeffer
Arnst	Ikstadt	Scherer
Becker	Kaiser	Schiller
Bopp	Karle	Schmiedt
Barbach	Köhler	Schneider
Dazenheim	Kräuter	Schütz
Fahl	Lieders	Simon
Freund	Maurer	Seitz
Geringer	Michel	Trieber
Grün	Neff	Trippel
Hart	Neumann	Vogt
Heiland	Nicolausen	Werner
Hermann	Nillmayer	Will
Hess	Popp	Zeichmann

Darrel Philip Kaiser

Moscow's
Final Solution:
The Genocide
of the
German-Russian
Volga Colonies

Darrel Philip Kaiser

Religions
of Germany
and the
German-Russian
Volga Colonies

Darrel Philip Kaiser

The Bad
and
Downright Ugly
of the
German-Russian
Volga Colonies

Darrel Philip Kaiser

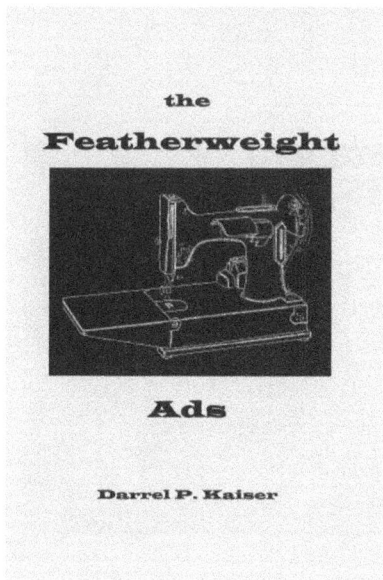

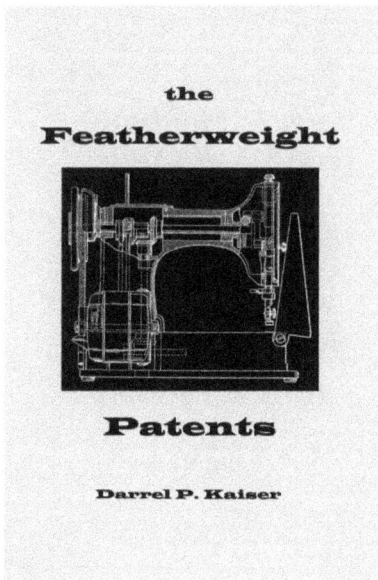